Marketing Magic

The Bigger Bang for the Smaller Budget

Ralf Bieler

DASH POINT PUBLISHING

Federal Way, Washington

Marketing Magic
The Bigger Bang for the Smaller Budget

by Ralf Bieler

Published by:
Dash Point Publishing, Inc.
P.O. Box 25591
Federal Way, WA 98093-2591 U.S.A.

All Rights Reserved. No part of this book may be reproduced or transmitted in any form or by any means, electronic or mechanical, including photocopying, recording or by any information storage and retrieval system, without written permission from the author, except for the inclusion of brief quotations in a review.

©2004, 2005 by Ralf Bieler

ISBN, print edition   1-889095-09-5
ISBN, eBook edition   1-889095-10-9

Names of people and companies in this book are used as examples or have been intentionally changed. Any similarity between these names and names of actual people and companies is unintended and purely coincidental.

While every reasonable attempt has been made to obtain accurate information, the author and publisher hereby disclaim any liability for problems due to errors, omissions, or changed information in this publication.

Portions of this book were printed in *Marketing Tools for Small Factors and Consultants* by Jeff Callender ©2004, 2005. Used by permission.

Printed in the United States of America.

Library of Congress Control Number 2004109363

Dedication

To Flor

Without your endless patience, unconditional support, wise guidance, and candid critique along the way, this book would have never been written, nor would I have likely accomplished many other things during the last 21 years. Thank you for being my best friend, my true companion, my dedicated partner, and my loving wife.

Also by Ralf Bieler

Marketing Resource Kit
Includes:
- The fully animated, professional, state-of-the-art PowerPoint Presentation that wins the business
- Your Brochure template: sample creative & persuasive copy
- Your Ad/Flyer template: sample creative & persuasive copy
- Power-letter to small company
- Power-letter to large company
- Engaging phone script (small company)
- Engaging phone Script (large company)
- The exactly right answers to the toughest cost questions & objections
- Build rapport while pre-qualifying (phone or face-to-face discussion guide)
- **Marketing Magic** – *The Bigger Bang for the Smaller Budget* (the e-Book)

Available from www.DashPointPublishing.com

Contents

Contents 5
About the Author 7
Important Notice 9
Acknowledgments 11
Preface 13

INTRODUCTION 15
1. What Is Marketing? 17

HOW-TO'S 21
2. Secrets to More Effective Marketing 23
3. Your Key to Success: Communication 31
4. How to Get More Out of a Phone Call 39
5. Answering Questions and Objections about Cost 53
6. The Art of Marketing and Advertising 57
7. The Marketing Plan: Your Way to El Dorado 61

PRACTICAL MATTERS 71
8. Marketing Versus Selling 73
9. What Works or Doesn't Work (for Us)? 75
10. Marketing Time and Budget 97
11. Does Size Matter? 101
12. Presentations 109
13. Recommendations 111

CLOSING 117
14. Final Comments 119

APPENDIX 121
Sample Call Script for Small to Midsize Companies 123
Sample Letter to Prospects in Small to Midsize Companies 129
What Readers Are Saying 132
Order Page 134

About the Author

Ralf Bieler
Multiple Funding Solutions, Inc.
18729 SE Lakeside Way
Tequesta, FL 33469
Phone: (561) 746-1954
Fax: (561) 658-6275
Email: info@multiplefundingsolutions.com
Web Site: www.multiplefundingsolutions.com

Ralf Bieler is one of the two principals and the CEO of Multiple Funding Solutions, Inc., a Florida corporation that started in November 2002. With his wife and partner Flor, he spent the first six months setting up the company, planning the business, and getting the initial marketing coordinated and under way. The Bielers funded their first client in May 2003 and became members of ACFA's "Million Dollar Club" ten months later in March 2004.

Multiple Funding Solutions, Inc. specializes in business planning, consulting, and financing new and established small to midsize companies. Their core business is Factoring and PO Funding; they buy small receivables up to about $50,000. Multiple Funding Solutions, Inc. also helps with other cash flow instruments and most other forms of traditional and creative business financing, some of which require a professional business plan before any funding decisions are made. Business plans are provided through the consulting arm of the business.

Their key mission is making small to mid-sized companies more successful by identifying and implementing creative business building, management, and financing solutions that are user friendly and produce tangible top and bottom line results.

Besides his role as Principal and CEO of Multiple Funding Solutions, Inc., Ralf is also the President and co-founder of Factor Solutions, Inc., a Florida corporation specializing in the development of innovative business management software solutions, web sites, company logos, as well as marketing and training resources for Consultants and Factors.

Ralf also serves on the Board of Directors of various other companies in non-related industries and has received the 2003 "You Make the Difference" award from the Business Loan Fund of the Palm Beaches for valuable contributions to their business development programs.

Having lived and worked in many countries around the world for most of his professional life in international business, marketing, and advertising since 1983, Ralf's expertise includes a broad portfolio of business and marketing solutions typically required for managing a multinational Fortune 500 business. Special areas of his expertise include strategic Marketing and Brand Management, and Communication and Advertising development.

He held various executive positions such as International Director, Senior Vice President, and Executive Vice President for some of the world's leading global research and consulting organizations. As a member of the European business management team, he was part of a Fortune 100 company's core business divisions with responsibility for Market Research, New Market Development, and Relationship Marketing.

Ralf has published several articles on sales volume forecasting and general research practices and written a series of factoring book reviews. He has had keynote speaker, presentation, and teaching/training engagements at numerous Fortune 500 consumer goods industry conferences in the USA, Europe, and Asia, as well as for the American Marketing

Association, the S.C.O.R.E. group, and a non-profit business development and financing organization in Florida.

Raised in Germany with most of his education completed in Europe, Ralf holds the equivalent of a Business and Administration degree with a concentration in Marketing and Communication. He was first introduced to Factoring in 1996 during his professional life in the UK.

Ralf and Flor were married in 1983. After moving from Germany to London, to Paris, to Connecticut, they have now settled down in a small hamlet close to Palm Beach, Florida. The few hours Ralf is not busy with his clients or businesses or helping consultants, he likes to spend in peace and quiet with Flor, socializing with friends, going to the movies, reading, playing racquet ball or scuba diving.

Important Notice

This publication is for educational purposes only and is not intended to give legal, tax, or professional advice. If such service is needed, the reader should seek professional advice from a competent attorney or accountant.

The author and publisher assume no responsibility for any financial losses a reader may experience as a result of any factoring or other business or investment transaction.

Acknowledgments

Thank you...

Jeff, for your inspiration, your never-ending persistence in pushing me further and further, and for all your help and guidance through the maze of a million or so technical details it took to get this show on the road. And thank you for your outstanding job of editing this book and for finally getting it published and into print. Without you *Marketing Magic* would have still just been another manuscript in my drawer and would have probably never seen the light of day. I'm grateful for your help and support, but fortunate and blessed to have you as a trusted friend and partner.

Trisha, for lending me a second and third pair of eyes and for catching so many of my initial mistakes that it was embarrassing. Of course, now I can and shamelessly will always blame you, if there are still a few boo-boos left in the book. What a great relief!

Rex, for taking the time to provide me with your brilliant ideas on how to improve certain passages and chapters.

And last but not least, **to all you consultants and factors** out there, who have bombarded me with all your questions over time, and who have helped me better understand what issues in our line of business are of utmost concern to you. I hope I have addressed and structured them in a way beneficial to you.

Preface

Given the key role marketing plays in any factoring and consulting operation, I have never understood why so little was written about it for so long. In my book *Marketing Tools for Small Factors and Consultants: A Hands-on Guide to Methods That Work*, Ralf Bieler shared some of his very helpful insights about marketing in general, and marketing for factors and consultants in particular.

His many years of success in the business world, his expertise and unbridled enthusiasm for marketing, and his quick success in the cash flow industry, together make his insights and perspective both unique and highly valuable.

What you are holding, *Marketing Magic – The Bigger Bang for the Smaller Budget,* is an unabridged guide to marketing for small factors and consultants. This book goes well beyond descriptive "what to do" recommendations and deep into demonstrations of "how to do it right" in order to increase your success.

The benefit of *Marketing Magic* to you, the reader, is the full perspective from a true expert in the industry as to how to market your business successfully with even the smallest budget. Typically complex and complicated marketing models are broken down and illustrated or explained in common terms for the marketing expert and non-expert alike. The ideas are easy to understand and implement into your own operation; doing so will make you more skilled and proficient, and your marketing efforts more effective and less costly.

So with great pleasure I present this book that explains, from A to Z, one of the most important aspects of running your factoring or consulting operation. I am confident it will help bring about your personal success as well as the success of your business.

Jeff Callender

Introduction

*"It's not just what you do,
it's how you do it."*

1.

What Is Marketing?

During twenty years of my "previous life" working in international business, marketing, and advertising with many Fortune 500 companies and their advertising agencies, the concept of marketing has always intrigued me and continues to do so today. During the early days I was fortunate to learn from numerous high-caliber marketers and experts in the consumer goods industry – the industry that basically "invented" marketing.

As definitions and practices of marketing – and particularly good marketing – vary and evolve over time, the conceptual "gestalt" of marketing is not always as clear cut as one might expect. To create a comprehensive picture of marketing, one has to see the multi-faceted nature of this discipline that is split up into hundreds of little pieces, like a puzzle, which – only when put together properly – provide a clear image of what is depicted. As I have often witnessed and sometimes helped create the magic that will come about when the image is properly assembled, I felt compelled to put this puzzle together and to develop an understanding of marketing that works for me and will hopefully be equally useful for many others in our industry. This background and the objective of sharing the learning and experiences became the driving force for writing this book.

In fact, the essence of marketing is quite simple, yet perhaps not as obvious as it may seem.

The Merriam-Webster dictionary defines marketing as "1a: the act or process of selling or purchasing in a market, and 1b: the process or technique of promoting, selling, and distributing a product or service. 2: an aggregate of functions involved in moving goods from producer to consumer.

The Encyclopedia Britannica offers a similar explanation: "Marketing's principal function is to promote and facilitate exchange. Through marketing, individuals and groups obtain what they need and want by exchanging products and services with other parties."

For practical purposes, I find these definitions useful only to an extent. They help us understand that Marketing is more than just a single event or activity. We see words like process, technique, promoting, selling, needs, and wants; all directed towards the single purpose of "exchanging goods or services with other parties." So, we understand that the overall purpose of marketing is somehow related to selling. What we don't really glean from these definitions though, is a good understanding of how all of these puzzle pieces fit together and what really creates the "magic" in the end.

In reality, marketing is comprised of many ongoing activities that encompass a lot of different things. Marketing includes planning and budgeting, strategy development and tactical implementation, targeting, branding, pricing, positioning, packaging, advertising, promotion, and amassing competitive intelligence. It's about differentiation. It's about defining your own USP (unique selling proposition) that lets you rise above the rest and makes you stand out among the crowd of like-minded people who are chasing the same dream – and ultimately the same customer.

But in order for your marketing to be successful, you need more than just this initial understanding of what Marketing entails. You need to understand and define your overall business and product or service objectives, as well as the size and the dynamics of the market you want to conquer. You need to uncover the needs and wants of your customers, and you need to anticipate your competitors' plans and actions, but also their reactions to anything you plan and do.

Your plans and strategies must be sound and realistic. Solid financial plans and projections that show the intended budget you will spend and the return you are likely to achieve are a key cornerstone in any strategy and plan. But you must also be able to execute it with the resources available to you. There is no point in making a brilliant plan if you don't have the money or other resources or the determination and resolve to carry it out.

If the ultimate purpose of marketing is to better sell your products or services, then it really doesn't matter whether you are a small business owner or chairman of a mega-corporation. As long as you interact with others, and as long as you communicate with them in order to do what you do, you are involved in marketing.

In other words, no matter what you do, as long as it is visible or audible to the outside world, you're marketing. You are doing something that creates a perception of you and your business. And the perception you create better be in line with the perception you want to create! One of my previous bosses – the president in a Fortune 100 company at the time – once said:

"Marketing is not a corporate function or department, but the responsibility of each and every one of our employees worldwide, no matter what their day job is."

So, the real question is not about whether or not you like marketing or whether you think it is or is not for you. If you want to be successful in this industry – or for that matter, in any business in which you are at the helm of the company – the **real question is how to get your marketing right, and how to improve it as you move along.**

And since available budgets typically play a role in marketing, we constantly have to think of new and more creative ways of bringing about "marketing success" and creating that "magic" that everyone is hoping to achieve. **The real art of the game is to make limited budgets work harder and to get "a bigger bang for our bucks."** The real job is to create that "magic" with as much investment as necessary, but with as little as possible.

How-To's

"By sailing your ship close to familiar shores, you will never discover new continents."

2.

Secrets to More Effective Marketing

Relationship Marketing

The smartest marketers nowadays build relations or form strategic alliances with other companies that sell "complementary" products or services, whose "image" fits well with their own product or service. By cross-promoting and cross-advertising together, both companies can save big on marketing support dollars, while creating more awareness and an even better image for each of their products or services through reciprocal endorsement. It's called "Relationship Marketing": a very powerful tool and a very smart move, as long as the products or services

- target the same customer
- do not compete
- are a good fit and can cross-fertilize each other
- have a good and similar image

How does this work in our industry? Let's say you work in Cash Flow and provide access to Factoring or Purchase Order Funding dollars. You might "team up" with someone who specializes in writing business plans for his customers. You can easily market to the same customer, since you both provide the type of services he will need to capitalize his business. Yet you do not compete, because you are offering two very distinct services.

Let's assume both of you did the same amount of marketing for your own service. By cross-promoting each other, you would immediately double your marketing reach without any extra costs to either of you. You can probably think of many other "good fits" with your business that could equally increase your marketing reach and effectiveness in the very same way!

The point here is that **through "team marketing" smaller players can achieve greater success by combining their efforts.**

In essence, everything we do that is somehow "visible" or "audible" to the outside world has a marketing effect, intended or not. And it's not only **what** we do, it's often much more **how** we do it.

So, what's the secret of good marketing? There are many, but here is an overview of what it takes to elevate your marketing success to new heights:

- Segment the market
- Determine your niche, and focus on it
- Decide what you want to stand for (your positioning)
- Decide to whom you are going to market

- Define your ICP (ideal customer profile) as precisely as possible
- Understand the needs and expectations of your ideal customer
- Understand how to communicate with your ideal customer to be:
  - Relevant to him/her
  - Different from your competitors
  - Credible
- Don't try to be everything to everybody; it usually never works.

Now, let's look at all this a little more closely to better understand what is really involved in getting from a general roadmap to a more detailed, action-oriented plan and to what we need to do to execute it:

Seven Steps to Superior Marketing

1. **Define your business**: What exactly do you offer (the "supply")? Define it from the perspective of your customer, and focus on the benefits to the customer more than on the sheer features of your product or service. For example, when you specialize in Factoring, you don't just offer "quick access to unlimited funds" (who would believe this anyway?). Instead, you could offer "smart financing solutions that let you grow your business with peace of mind and without additional debts."

2. **Define your market** (the "demand"): Who wants what you offer? This should include a very precise definition of **your "ideal customer."** Be careful and think at least twice: defining your market is tricky. How you define your market will dictate how you build your marketing plan and what your marketing message is! If you were in the business of selling milk, would your target market be "milk drinkers"? "Non-milk drinkers"? "People who are thirsty"?

"Health fanatics"? "Cat owners"? "Families with kids"? "Everybody"?

Remember, the more precisely you define your target market and ideal customers, the better you will be able to "communicate" with them. For a good definition of your market and ideal customer, consider all of the following questions, in order to get a very precise picture of your marketing focus and what tools you need to use to reach your ideal customers:

- What are their distinctive socio-demographic characteristics?
- What industry/business are they in?
- What is their company profile (e.g. annual sales, number of employees, type of customers, etc.)?
- Where are they (geographically dispersed or clustered)?
- What are the symptoms, issues, questions, problems, opportunities, anxieties, etc. they have (and have in common!) that make your product/service desirable to them?
- Who do you need to reach for the decision making process?
- How easy is it for you to reach your "ideal customers," and how will you do it?
- How would you briefly and precisely describe them to someone else so he/she knows whom to refer to you, how to recognize them, and where to find them?
- How many of these companies/customers exist (Size of your target market)?

3. **Prioritize your ideal customer groups**, and define their individual needs and requirements separately. Yes, you can have more than one ideal customer group! Just don't treat them or market to them as if they were all the same! And don't market to all of them at the same time. You need different communication and perhaps different strategies to

reach them. If you do it all at the same time, it can easily get way too complex for a small business like yours. It is much better to focus on one group at a time.

4. **Define how you want to be perceived** by your ideal customer group(s) (your positioning); this should be the same across different customer groups! You can't be the "premium brand" to some, and the "value offer" to others under the same name. It's not credible. If you want to market to both segments, do it under different [brand/company] names. A "Rolls Royce compact economy" at the price of a Honda Civic is not a credible market proposition.

5. **Define exactly why your ideal customer(s) want to work with you.** Are you the only one from whom they can get this service or buy this product? If not, what do they get from you that they can't get from your competition? Or, why are the benefits you offer better than what your competitors offer?

6. **Define how you will reach your ideal customer(s).** Will you reach them directly, or perhaps through others who might have a better way of reaching your ideal customer than you?

7. **Define your message and communication strategy** for each of your ideal customer groups separately. For example, what do you tell "the milk drinker" vs. "the non-milk drinker" vs. "the thirst-quencher"? The first one will need reassurance why he should buy his milk from you (what are your benefits vs. other milk vendors?). The second one will need to be "persuaded" why he should change his current behavior and start drinking milk all of a sudden (what benefits has he been missing by not drinking milk?). And the third will need to be convinced that milk quenches thirst better than any other beverage (you're not competing only with other milk vendors anymore). You see why your communication must be different for these three groups? Do you have credible arguments and reasons for

all three of them, or can you perhaps really make a case for only one or two of them? If you can't make a case for a particular group, don't market to them. They are not your ideal customer!

Now, how do we apply all this to the cash flow industry? What would such a plan look like in our line of business? Here is a simplistic example of what it could be for a fictitious small factoring company called Business Financing Partners, or BFP for short:

Which business am I in (business definition)?
Via Accounts Receivable purchasing, BFP specializes in providing a smart financing solution that let you run and grow your business with peace of mind without creating additional debts.

Which market am I serving (market definition)?
BFP provides this business financing solution to new and established small and midsize companies on a national level. These companies are defined as businesses with annual sales between $60,000 and $600,000, who want/need to sell receivables between $2,500 and $25,000 per month (i.e., roughly 50% of sales). They typically have between 1 – 10 employees and sell their products or services to a roster of well established, creditworthy customers. Primary target industries are staffing agencies and private investigators, secondary target industries comprise all manufacturing companies. Both primary and secondary targets have a demonstrated need for bi-weekly cash injections, which they require a) to meet their payroll obligations or b) to expand their operations. Their customers are reliable and pay their invoices, but typically exceed their 30-days payment terms. BFP's ideal customers are nationally dispersed (no geographic clusters exist) and are run/owned by individuals between 35 and 55 years of age with average to above average education. Key contacts for BFP are

the business owners. There is a national total of about x million companies that fit these criteria.

Who are my key priority customers?
Prior to a regional and subsequent national roll-out of BFP services, the key customer focus will be on those companies at a local level and within a radius of x miles from BFP premises. The size of this initial market segment is roughly x hundred potential businesses. Initial marketing will focus on staffing agencies, followed by private investigators, and finally manufacturing companies.

Targeted perception / positioning of BFP
The market will perceive BFP as the ultimate, desired, and trusted service partner in the area of short-term business financing. BFP is the loyal friend, the trusted partner, and the helping hand, which is always just a phone call or e-mail away.

Why do our "ideal customers" want to work with BFP?
Our positioning will be visibly demonstrated by our client-centered approach and will be supported by our commitment to and understanding of the business and personal needs and objectives of our customers, as well as by the personal touch and superior knowledge that BFP employees constantly bring into each relation. The extent and quality of our services will be unmatched, and our financing programs will be customized to our client-partners' needs. Our core commitment to only delivering value-added solutions will determine our business practices. Targeted customer response: "There is no one who understands us as well and helps us as much as BFP."

How will I reach my "ideal customers"?
Initial contact with the business owners will be primarily established via phone and mail/e-mail, based on addresses purchased or copied from local phone directories/Yellow Pages. Word-of-mouth, networking groups, and third party referrals from consultants as well as from existing and

prospective clients will further aid to build the awareness, positioning, and reach of BFP.

BFP communication strategy
a) <u>For target companies that are in a turn-around mode:</u>
All BFP communication will focus on the benefits that factoring will have on eliminating the business problems and the fear of "not making it." Key issues to address are the here and now, such as meeting payroll on time, keeping taxes current, not getting behind on accounts payable, etc.

b) <u>For target companies that are in a growth mode:</u>
All BFP communication will focus on the benefits that factoring can have on the acceleration of business growth, the opportunity to hire new sales reps, accept larger orders, command better vendor terms, etc. The key issue to address is the better future and the ease with which the business owner can focus completely on growing his business, instead of being held back by the lack of sufficient funds.

Now, remember, the previous section is a fictitious plan for a fictitious company called BFP. It took about one hour to think about it and write it as is. It is not meant to serve as an exhaustive plan for your business. Instead, the plan is merely meant to illustrate the process and the questions that you should answer and how you might answer them (in writing!) for yourself and your business. Developing and writing your plan will take much longer! The above plan is simply a blueprint you can follow, but in order for it to work for you, you will need to determine for yourself what goes in there. It must make sense for you, your business, and how you want to run it. It must reflect your own personality, your own style, and your own ideas. If you simply copied what is here, you would be missing the point and taking a shortcut that might not take your business where it should go.

With this in mind, and while important, let's look at what will eventually be your biggest single contributor to your future marketing success.

*"If you keep doing what you've done,
you'll keep getting what you've got."*

3.

Your Key to Success: Communication

If you only read or remember one chapter of this book, read and remember this one! Getting your communication right will make the single biggest difference in your marketing success.

The messages and communication you choose must be relevant, important, and credible to your target market. If your ideal customer can identify with your offer and how it's being presented, you have done a great marketing job already and an important battle of your "marketing war" is already won.

Good marketing really boils down to one thing: Segmented and targeted communication. It's as simple as that. Why communication? Think about how you market your business. What are the tools you use? Business cards, web site, brochures, presentations, networking, direct mail, flyers, magazine/newspaper articles, public speaking, press releases, advertising, face-to-face or phone conversations, etc. Have you noticed? All these marketing tools are about communication!

Why segmented? Because you should not use the same lingo and jargon with everybody. **You need to adapt what you say and how you say it to whomever is listening**. Everybody has a different frame of reference and understanding, and you want to make sure you're understood properly, no matter with whom you are speaking.

Why targeted? Because **only targeted communication allows you to be relevant and credible to those you want to reach.** Remember: communication reaches its peak effectiveness when what you say is relevant to your target audience. And what is more relevant to your target audience than their own individual questions, concerns, issues, and problems? So **make your targeted communication about them!**

To really understand marketing, you therefore need to understand communication. How does it really work, and what does it take to communicate?

In order to communicate, you need more than one party (unless you're into soliloquies). Ideally one speaks and others listen and/or watch. **The objective of communication is to get the intended message from the sender to the recipients**.

What else does it take? **You need attention**. Think about communication as a radio or TV broadcast. A station can broadcast as much as it likes, But if no one tunes in, the broadcast doesn't reach anybody, and no matter how exciting the messages in the broadcast are, no one will get them. So **in order to communicate you need your audience to "tune in."**

Have you ever watched a foreign TV station? It can be quite entertaining. You somehow understand what a show is all about, but chances are you have no idea what is being said. You can tell if the actors are happy or sad, nervous or relaxed. But when it comes to the dialogue, you're totally lost. No matter how hard you try to "tune in," you have no clue what they are saying simply because you do not understand the language.

The point is that attention or **"tuning in" is not enough**, if the message is sent in a language you don't understand. If you are listening, is it your fault therefore, if you don't get it? Not necessarily. If the sender of the message wants to reach you, it is his or her responsibility to convey the message in a language you understand.

Language is a code the sender uses to get a message across. The recipient of the message must first decode the message in order to understand it. So when you "code" a message you want your ideal customer to "get," the code you use must be easily understood by your recipient. If not, well, your "broadcast" might be entertaining, but you're certainly not communicating.

Isn't this too obvious? Perhaps, but aren't you often surprised how easily this simple prerequisite of good communication gets overlooked, involuntarily or on purpose? You don't even have to use a foreign language. Just talk to any local "specialist" in a certain field. How many times have you talked with a doctor or a lawyer – or for that matter – a financial advisor? Can you honestly say you understood everything they said when they used professional lingo or jargon? You will probably feel much more comfortable and trust them more when they use terminology you understand. When they speak "your language," i.e., when you understand them, you automatically "feel" they are a good doctor, lawyer, or financial advisor.

Let's say you know what code or language to use when addressing your audience. **How do you get them to "tune in" to what you have to say?** Ideally, you **make them aware of your intention to "broadcast" before you even start**, and you let them know that your message will contain something important and relevant to them. Let me repeat the most important words here: **RELEVANT TO THEM**.

In other words, you **create interest and attention before "spilling the beans."** For example, in a group situation, people often talk on top of each other at the same time. Somebody throws out a question to which you have the perfect answer. You shout it out but nobody reacts, because nobody took notice; they were all talking at the same time and not listening.

Instead of shouting out your answer, **try asking a question**. You might say something like *"Would you care to hear a good solution for this?"* Chances are that the group chatter will cease and heads will turn your way, even if you only wanted to address one single person. Why? Because you are asking a question and intuitively people will want to answer it! This is how we have been socially conditioned. And of course, "No" would not be a socially acceptable answer in this situation, since most of us have also been trained in common courtesy and will conform to social norms.

Now you've got their attention. This is the time to present your solution. But you better make sure it is relevant to them. What if you don't know what's relevant to them? Find out before you start communicating! Otherwise, all your good efforts may go wasted (and you're back to monologues because no one "tunes in").

How do you find out what's relevant to your audience? Study them and learn as much about them as you can. **The easiest way of finding out what is relevant to them is to ask them!**

Avoid making assumptions. Assumptions are typically based on your own frame of reference and experiences in life and in business. For any one person, this is unfortunately still a rather limited "data base" to analyze and from which to draw conclusions. Making assumptions is a bit like gambling: Sometimes you get it right, but in the long run you always lose. When we make an assumption, we often tend to treat it as reality, because it just seems so logical, so clear, and so obvious to us. But everybody else's reality, logic, and perspective might in fact be very different from our own. It's the old story with the glass of water that is "**only** half full"…or is it **still** half full…or **already** half empty? Which of the three is a positive or optimistic perspective, and which one is rather negative and pessimistic? Well, that will depend entirely on whether the desired result would be a full or an empty glass! You see why the "right" answer will always depend on the perspective?

Lucky for us, some general assumptions in business have already proven to be true and are pretty safe. They are therefore no longer "assumptions" but hard facts. What is more relevant to a business owner than the success of his or her business? In general, you will find **six things that – individually or in combination – are always the hot buttons for any business owner:**

1. How to maximize the "top line" (sales)
2. How to maximize the "bottom line" (profit)
3. How to generate profitable growth over time
4. How to decrease cost
5. How to improve productivity (efficiency: the result/cost ratio)
6. How to increase effectiveness (how to produce better results)

If you **link these hot buttons to solutions you and your service can provide**, you can be sure to win a lot of hearts, and your communication (marketing) will always be relevant.

How do you know which one or more of the six hot buttons are most important to a prospect at a certain time? If you don't know already from your previous information or research, there's only one way to find out. Ask:

- *"What is the best thing you wish would happen in your business right now or in the very near future, and what would it take to get there?"*
- Or, *"What would be the ideal situation your business could be in right now or in the near future, and what would need to happen to achieve this?"*

- Or, *"If you prioritized the things that would most benefit your business right now, what would be the most important one?"*
- Or, *"What is the single biggest challenge your business is currently facing, and what exactly needs to happen to turn this around?"*
- Or, *"If you could make one thing go away that negatively affects your business right now, what would that be and how could it be fixed?"*
- Or, *"If you could improve one thing in your business right now, what would that be, and what needs to happen to improve it?"*

Notice how the first three questions focus on "good things" and use "positive" words, whereas the last three questions address "problems" and use "negative" language that points towards a positive outcome.

When a business is on the up-swing and growing, the mood in the company is positive and optimistic. In these cases, choose one of the first three questions (or something similar), because they enforce the positive momentum.

However, when the company is in "survival mode" and is struggling, the mood is somber and morale is down. In these cases, choose one of the bottom three questions (or something similar), because they address the reality and point to a better future.

I call this **situation-congruence**. Being situation-congruent means you've listened, you understand, you are empathetic, and you care. You're in sync with the people and communicate with them in a fashion that is relevant to their specific situation.

Not being situation-congruent is like telling the most hilarious jokes at a funeral, or trying to discuss the world's most serious problems at a wild and crazy New Year's Eve party. It only shows how much you care about yourself or the things that are important to you. It does not demonstrate any compassion for those you interact with. It is all about you.

Have you ever noticed how many sales people focus their communication only on themselves (their company) and their products or services? They know and tell you everything about their own product or service, how great it is, what specifications it has, what features it contains, etc. However, they often don't close the loop by demonstrating "what's in it for you." In other words, they don't **focus on the benefits for the customer**, but only talk about the features of their own product or service whether you have a need for it or not.

What happens when you find yourself at the receiving end of such "communication"? Don't you just wish they would leave you alone and move on to their next target? Do you really want to listen to them, or do you become impatient, bored, or maybe even annoyed? Is your mind not already trying to come up with a plausible excuse for how to best get rid of these "sales hyenas"?

Your customers will feel the same, if everything they hear from you is all about you and your product or service!

From this chapter you can glean the added benefit of your understanding and following the process of good communication. You have seen examples of how easily good and more effective communication can be accomplished: simply ask a lot of questions instead of making bold statements about your own products or services, and focus your communication on what is relevant to your audience.

Now, let's dig a little deeper and look at how this can be accomplished in conversations on the phone – or for that matter in any dialogue with your prospective and existing customers.

4.
How to Get More Out of a Phone Call

Let's look at common telemarketing practices for a moment, because telemarketing – or "cold calling" – is often used but frequently "abused." Some people believe in it, others don't. In some industries or business sectors it works, in others it does not, and some customer segments are more receptive than others. In any case, there are a lot of things we can learn by looking closely at telemarketing and its common practices:

> *"Hello, Sir, I'm calling you to let you know that our company has decided to provide you the opportunity to consolidate all your credit card balances into one account with no transfer charges and at a 0% interest rate for the first six months. We do this because you are one of our most valued customers. It's great, because it doesn't cost you anything right now, and there is no hassle. Let me just verify your address and contact details. OK? This call may be monitored for quality purposes. OK?"*

No, it's not OK at all! There's a lot wrong with this approach! The caller typically doesn't even know your current credit card situation, nor does he or she bother to find out or ask. You may be perfectly happy with your current credit card balances, and not need this service at all. Instead of finding this out and starting to create a need, the "annoying telemarketer" just delves right in and "assumes" (here's that bad word again!) he has something that is of interest to you.

The caller reads from a standard script and talks at the speed of light and with so little intonation or pause that it's sometimes hard to understand what he actually wants. If you ask a question, he typically just starts re-reading from the script again, instead of answering what you asked.

You're one of their "most valued customers"? Most of the time they can't even pronounce your name or have no idea who you are.

As a "valued customer" the caller needs to verify your address and tape the conversation? Don't you know who your valued customers are, where they live, and what they need? Do you need to tape your conversations with them for "quality purposes"? Would the quality of your service increase, if you started taping the phone calls with your clients?

Well, of course, everybody knows why they do that and how telemarketing works. But still, how does it make you feel when you are at the receiving end? Intrigued by their offer? Indifferent? Or worse?

As a matter of fact, most telemarketers don't really know anything about your needs or you at all. Your name and phone number simply happens to be on their address list. Yet, they pretend and feed you with empty phrases and lines that obviously serve only one purpose: to make you say "yes" and ultimately make you buy whatever it is they're offering. Are they creating the trust they need to entice you and interest you in their product or service?

Now, don't get me wrong. From a marketing perspective, there's nothing wrong with telemarketing at all. Legislation – at least for the private sector – disagrees, of course, and the ever increasing amount of numbers on the do-not-call lists is living proof of the invasive nature of the beast and how people actually feel about it. But again, from a marketing perspective, it certainly has its place and reason for being. Otherwise it wouldn't exist, and people would have long given up using it without the need for legislative pressure. In fact, this is another irrefutable law of any marketing activity: If it's not working, fix it. And if it can't be fixed, drop it.

But how can telemarketing be "fixed"? Let's think of a very simple scenario. You want to use telemarketing (or cold calling) for your own business. How can **you** make it work for you and achieve better results (or at least not annoy so many people you contact)? Try a relatively simple approach:

1. **Define the outcome** you want to achieve with a first phone call. Tip: "selling" or even closing a deal is not a good objective. More reasonable objectives are to:
   - <u>briefly</u> introduce yourself
   - get to know your prospect
   - become familiar with and understand his/her situation, issues, concerns, needs, values, experiences, etc.
   - let your prospect know what your clients expect from you (their benefits!)
   - build rapport
   - create curiosity about what you offer
   - set up a meeting

   And by no means would I suggest that you should accomplish all of these in your first call. Just pick one! And then cover the next one(s) in subsequent conversations.

   Some people will even argue this is already way too ambitious for the first contact. One theory suggests that the only purpose of making the first call is to make the first call.

2. **Prepare and use a script** until you feel perfectly comfortable to "fly blind." Tip: good scripts are loaded with questions about the prospect, not with statements about you and your product or service. A good rule: talk 20%, listen 80%. If you have to use statements, use those

that are general in nature and with which everybody would agree. Remember, you want to avoid early disagreement!

3. **Write down the possible answers** to your questions, and prepare follow-up questions to those answers. Tip: use questions that make both "yes" and "no" answers a desirable outcome. Make sure that a yes or no answer does not close the door for the follow-up, or worse, that it leaves you no room to continue the conversation. Follow-up with open-ended "why," "what," and "how" questions. This is where you get the most important information, as it helps you understand your contact's true motivation. Often a simple *"hmm, that's interesting. Tell me more about that"* can go a long way in gathering information and building rapport at the same time.

4. **Before you pick up the phone**, gather as much information as possible on the company you are about to call. Familiarize yourself with what they do, their products or services, who their competitors are, and what typical issues their industry or business is facing. Do your homework! It pays off.

5. **When you're on the phone**, make sure you get "permission" to talk with your contact at a time that's convenient for them. For example, before you jump right in or continue with your spiel, ask them, if it is a good time to talk, or if they would prefer you to call them back at another time. Show that you respect their time and schedule!

6. **Whatever you talk about**, make sure it is <u>relevant, important, and of interest to your contact</u>. If in doubt, ask! If it's not relevant, important, or interesting to them, refrain from talking about it – no matter how much you want to. Do not try to convince them that it must be relevant, important, or interesting to them, just because it's relevant, important, or interesting to you. In fact, lead the conversation in a way that <u>they</u> feel in the driver's seat. In other words, ask for their "permission" to talk about

something, <u>before</u> you start talking about it. Of course, there are many ways to phrase such questions, but here are a few examples of how you can go about it:

Relevance check:
- *"Have you had similar experiences in your business/industry?"*
- *"Does/has this happened to you/in your business (as well)?"*
- *"Can you see this happening in your business /industry?"*
- *"Have you noticed this (as well) in your business/industry"?*
- *"Could you/your business benefit from....?"*

Importance check:
- *"Is this important to you/your business at the moment?"*
- *"How important is this for you/your business at this time"?*
- *"Is this something of concern for you/your business right now?"*

Interest check (and "permission to talk"):
- *"Would you like to hear more about this?"*
- *"Would you like me to cover this in more detail?"*
- *"Would you like me to explain this a little more?"*
- *"Is this something you'd like me to tell you about"?*
- *"Would you like me to tell you how this works?"*
- *"Would it help you to learn more about this"?*

7. **Practice paraphrasing** the typical "I" and "we" talk. It's somewhat difficult in the beginning, because we are not used to it, but it will be easy and quite natural after you try for a while. For example, instead of saying *"I can demonstrate how..."*, try *"you wanted to know how..."* (Assuming you have already established that this is something they wanted to know or talk about).

8. **Make sure that in every phone call** and during every contact you have with your prospect, you <u>always</u> agree on

"next steps" before saying good-bye. Never end a conversation without having a clear agreement with and commitment from your prospect on what needs to happen next, by when, and who is accountable for making it happen.

9. **Remember and make it clear to your prospect** that "No" is an acceptable answer. The point is, you can't really "sell" anything if there's no need. It's the old demand and supply thing. If there's no demand, it doesn't matter how much supply there is. In that case, supply has no value, so why are you trying to "sell"?

Why is "No" an acceptable or sometimes even a desirable answer? Simply because it's more efficient to get there quickly (so you can move on) than having your chain rattled for an extended period of time. When prospects tell you they need to think about it or are willing to accept but need to discuss it with others, or when they ask you to send them something in writing, most of the time, all they're really doing is stalling.

This sounds harsh and may be hard to believe, partly because we don't want to believe it. Instead we want to believe that we really had an interested prospect and that we're really going to close that deal sometime, but it will just take a little more work for us and time for them to convince others. But the truth is, more often than not, these prospects have either not understood the benefits of your offer, or they don't really care about it, or they are conceptually interested but want to shop around for better offers. More often than not, these situations are "time wasters" and are often a signal to move on to the next prospect.

If you use telemarketing or have experienced those stalling techniques before, try the following in your next call: Once you have opened the conversation and obtained permission to explain what it is you do and the related benefits, **tell the prospect what you do is not for**

everybody. The sole purpose of your call is to find out whether your service could be of benefit to them or their business. It's perfectly OK to say "No".

By the way, have you ever noticed how much more attractive almost anything becomes to children, when they are told that it's really **not** for them? And how much more reluctant they get, when you tell them that this is what they should do? Same thing! As soon as you can make people aspire to something, it has a higher perceived value.

If nothing else, such an approach will earn you more respect, may provide an opportunity to follow up later, or give you at least permission to ask them for a referral, in case your service is really not for them.

It's a fine way of closing such a conversation by saying *"Yes, I understand that having more working capital for your business is not what you need right now, but would it be OK for me to check back with you after some time to see if anything has changed? And perhaps you know someone you could refer me to, who might benefit from my services and more working capital right now?"*

If you have had a good and mutually respectful conversation with your prospect, and have been able to establish a decent rapport, they will be happy to refer you to someone else, even if their own business can't benefit from your service. Moreover, the person to whom you have been referred will not be another "cold call" for you! You already have a great "ice breaker" for your next call.

10. **Another important tip relates to expectation management**. When you move forward in your discussion with a prospect and possibly arrange the next meeting, make sure you set the agenda, and let him/her know what the intended outcome should be.

A nice and very effective way of summarizing this is:

"OK, we have agreed to meet on day x at time y at location z. Typically one of two things will

> *happen at the end of our meeting/conversation: You may either find that what I do is not for you, and that's OK, because it's really not for everybody. Or, you will like what you'll see/hear, and we will need to agree on the next steps to move forward."*

Make sure at the end of your meeting or next conversation, you come back to exactly these two alternatives, and insist the answer should really be one or the other. This is how you get commitment. Without commitment, chances are you never go anywhere with a prospect. Again, if it's a "No," don't forget to ask for a referral!

11. **Let's go back to the "why," "what," and "how" questions** for a moment. They not only provide the information about your contact's motivation; they also enable you to uncover and reinforce the _"relevant and real benefits"_ of your product or service _from your prospect's perspective_.

    This is a technique often used in psychology and in more refined market research approaches to uncover and understand deeply rooted values, beliefs, and motivations that do not appear on the surface. It is the old "iceberg" phenomenon, where only 20% is visible, but 80% of the "real thing" lies below the surface.

    This technique is referred to as "laddering." It allows you to understand and **move from features to factual benefits to emotional end benefits** (like climbing up a ladder: you can reach further when you're on top). It is important to understand the difference between the three and to use them appropriately when and where needed.

    - <u>A feature</u> is a simple characteristic a product or service possesses: *"The rates are very low."*
    - <u>A factual (a.k.a. rational) benefit</u> is what a feature does, while the feature itself may become the support

for the benefit: *"You can save a lot of money because the rates are very low."*

- **<u>An emotional end benefit</u>** brings a factual benefit to a higher level and taps into the real or ultimate desires, whereby the factual benefit may become the support, and the feature closes the loop and links it back to you: *"Imagine how you and your team would feel and where your business could go, if your sales and profits were up, while even saving a lot of money because of the low rates."*

Do you see the difference? A feature driven message is all about you or your service. By the time you get to the emotional end benefit, the message you are sending is all about your client or prospect! Which one do you think has the strongest marketing impact?

Emotional end benefits are the real hook, because they are what people are *<u>really</u>* looking for. However, they are hard to identify, because they are part of our innermost values and beliefs, and we don't really talk about them a lot, if at all. Sometimes we are not even consciously aware of them ourselves, or if we are, we may not want to share them freely. It takes some good skills to dig deep enough to get to that level. But it can and should be done, and is worth all the effort, if you want your marketing to double or triple in effectiveness.

Here is a simplified example of a conversation with a prospect (who is now a client by the way) using a "laddering" approach that illustrates how to get from a feature to an emotional end benefit in a normal conversation:

Q: From what you have just described, I understand there are plenty of business challenges for you right now. If we think in terms of priorities, what would be the most important or most beneficial result you want to achieve?

A: The most important thing right now is to find a way to have more money available **(Feature)**, since I can't get my bank to help me. They tell me I'm totally maxed out. **(Feature)**

Q: I hear that a lot. Many people tell me they need more money and can't get the bank to help them **(Use their words to summarize what they said to ensure you're always on the same page. I call this "reflection").** But tell me more about this. Why is this the most important and immediate priority for you, given everything else going on in your business?

A: Well, if I had the money right now, I could buy the materials needed to fill a big purchase order from this new customer and meet his timing requirements **(Factual Benefit)**. It's an important order for him, and I could really impress him, if I could do it in time **(Factual Benefit)**. He already told me that he's looking for a few reliable vendors, and he'd put me on his preferred vendor list, if this big order works out well for him **(Factual Benefit)**.

Q: So, if you could make it to this big customer's preferred vendor list **(Reflection)**, how exactly would you and your business benefit from that?

A: Well, you see, right now I'm struggling with a lot of smaller buyers. They're only buying sporadically and in smaller volumes. It's a lot of work and hassle, and I never really know how much is coming in each month. I can't afford to lose them, because they're my business so far **(Fear: Emotional End Benefit)**. But if I had more reliable orders from bigger clients, it would take out a lot of the day-to-day stress from the dependency on those smaller ones **(Emotional End Benefit)**. I'd be much more confident and relaxed about the way my business could grow **(Emotional End Benefit)**. It would be a great reference and enhance my image in the industry, if I had that big client on my client list **(Emotional End Benefit)**. Once you get one, the others are going to follow, and my business would be very successful in no time, which is what I always wanted **(Confidence & Gratification: Emotional End Benefits)**.

You see how we went from talking about a simple feature ("getting money") to a rich series of factual benefits and finally to an even more meaningful series of higher level emotional benefits.

You understand what makes your prospect really tick. How much more do you now know about his business and how he really feels? Now you can really help him achieve a much higher goal.

Of course, when he said he needed money, you could have jumped right in and offered a solution. But with the knowledge you have now, you are not only providing working capital to him for a short-term deal.

Instead you are now building his image in the industry and helping him achieve his long-term dream of independence. You are delivering success and profitable growth. You eliminate his day-to-day anxieties, instill long-term confidence, and bring instant gratification. Which one do you think makes the stronger and more effective marketing promise from his perspective?

To market successfully, you will need to learn at least two things:

1. How to make your communication (marketing) relevant and credible to your target audience
2. How to differentiate between "Features" and "Benefits" so your marketing messages become benefit driven

Transfer this example to features and benefits of your own product or service, and you're there. If you're not doing this already, use it, and you will see how much more effective you will become in being perceived as relevant, credible, and differentiated. You will have shifted the perception from a "service/product focus" to a "solution focus."

Service/Product Focus	Solution Focus
Provide information about your product or service	Seek information about customer business
Know everything about your product or service	Know your customer's business
Present your standard service	Develop solutions jointly with customer
Present product & pricing	Create solutions & value

Exercise: Before using this technique with prospects and clients in your business, practice it at home with your partner or spouse or friends. Don't tell them about it, but start and prolong each conversation by asking questions, instead of just making statements.

Good questions to ask are:

- *"Why is this important to you?"*
- *"If you could change one thing about...what would that be?"*
- *"How could this be changed to be more beneficial to you?"*
- *"How could it be made better?"*
- *"What would be the best possible outcome for you?"*
- *"What would need to take place in order for this to happen?"*
- *"Why do you say that?"*
- *"Why is that... (good/better/best or bad/worse)?"*
- *"What does/will this do for you?"*
- *"What is your greatest concern regarding ...?"*
- *"Help me understand this better..."*
- *"Interesting.... tell me more about this"*

Also use "Reflection": Use their words to summarize what they have just said, and follow this up with a question from the list:

"I understand that you ..... Tell me more about this. Why is that important to you?"

Another form of "Reflection" is using their statements and turning them into a (reflective!) question:

Partner says: *"I need to do this."*

You say: *"You need to do this? Why is that important to you?"*

Note that you can trigger different responses by putting the emphasis on different words in the first part of your question!

And don't be shy about repeating and combining some of the questions as your conversation moves on. It might feel strange for you in the beginning if you have never done this, but the more you practice, the more natural it becomes.

Your partner or friend will not notice it at all. In fact, if you do it every day and keep it up for a while, they will likely sense a positive change in the quality of their conversations with you and wonder how all of the sudden you have become such a good listener.

These "tips & tricks" are obviously not restricted to phone conversations only. They work equally well – if not better – in face-to-face situations as well. But when you are face-to-face with a prospect or a client, remember that there are other interactions that come into play, too.

Your appearance, your demeanor, and your body language will be equally important. **How** you come across should be perfectly congruent with **what** you say. Most signals that other people pick up, interpret, and use for their decision making process during a conversation are non-verbal, emotional cues.

But even if you do everything right, one of the barriers to "smooth sailing" into marketing success always remains and is likely to show its ugly face sooner or later: Objections from your prospect. One of the most common objections to almost anything in business life is the cost issue. No matter what it is you do or sell and regardless of the actual price, there will always be someone who claims it is too expensive. Our industry and business is no exception to this rule. How you can handle objections when marketing your factoring service is the subject of the next chapter.

*"To every difficult question
there is always an easy answer,
which is usually wrong"*

5.

Answering Questions and Objections about Cost

Another issue on the mind of many people when they are on the phone – or engaged in any face-to-face conversation with a prospect – is handling objections.

You've said all the right things, explained your service and its benefits to your prospect. He listened with interest and followed you wherever you took him. You're about to send him the application, and then it hits you out of the blue. "Yes, but….". Objection!

You better be prepared or all your previous efforts are lost. Objections can have two sources of origin: They are either true objections to something that does not make sense to your prospect and his business, or they are simply a polite pretense, indicating that your prospect does not feel comfortable with the general idea of the proposition and is looking for a "way out." But instead of being upfront about it, he disguises it as a "rational" objection or question, although his real motives are purely emotional.

Either way, you don't know what the real intention is at that point. One way of finding out is to "isolate" the objection and bring him back to a "commitment level."

A typical example is the price objection: *"This is really a great program, but unfortunately, it's way too expensive for me. My business simply can't afford it."*

You isolate the objection by responding: *"Yes, I can see why you would feel that way. In fact, many of my clients have voiced this concern in the beginning. But let's assume for a minute that we found a good solution on that front, would you then want to move forward?"*

If the concern was real and rational, his answer should be "yes," and you have established a new commitment. If it was an emotional pretense, he will find other "rational reasons," why your service is not for him, and chances are you're wasting your time.

If it is a real objection, chances are he may not have understood how factoring works and/or is confused about the "factoring fees." Let's say you've made the mistake of quoting a discount percentage too early, i.e., before you even had a chance to create a real value perception. Without a doubt, one of the most frequent objections is *"What? 5% for 30 days...? That's 60% interest per year!"*

If you need to respond – and yes, you do – here are a few examples of what you can say that may soften the blow and help bring your prospect back to the table:

1. You are not really *paying* **any** "fee" for using this service. It is a simple buy-sell process. I'm simply buying one of your assets (i.e., your accounts receivable) from you. And I'm paying **you** a price on which we mutually agree. The price I pay will depend – among other things – on how long an invoice is open, but how does that make **you** pay a fee?

2. Factoring is an off-balance-sheet financing tool, which does **not** create debt. It does **not** involve a traditional loan, so therefore you do not pay any interest at all.

3. You need to understand the difference between a "discount" and "interest". A discount of 5% on the face value of an invoice is like selling your product/service at 5% below its normal price. It is very different from taking a loan (i.e., going into debt) and paying 5% interest on it. They are completely different animals!

4. Factoring is a transaction-based, short-term financing tool, typically for no more than 90 days per transaction. Hence, the discount will never accumulate for a year, but typically for a maximum period of 90 days and most often less. But even if we assumed worst case scenario, a transaction with an invoice for $1,000 will still yield a total return of $850 after 90 days. But for that, you will have already received about $700 - $800 up-front, so you don't have to wait 90 days to get your money from your customer. Yes, in total you lost 3 x 5% or $150 of your return, but it has absolutely nothing to do with paying interest or paying a fee! It's really just like realizing a lower price on a sale during a promotion!

5. You can also think about it as a typical extension of terms: Most business people are happy to offer their customers a 2% net 10 discount! Why? Because they know it's more beneficial to discount the price by 2% than waiting 30 or 45 days to get paid. With 10 day terms, they could do 36 such transactions in a year. Would that equate to "paying 72% interest" or "paying a fee"? Of course, not! Nobody would even think about it that way!

6. Most people use factoring daily in their everyday life, but don't even realize or think about it. Think about a credit card transaction: no difference! You can pay for almost anything with a credit card these days. The

merchant accepts your credit card, but has to pay a transaction fee from anywhere between 2.5% - 4.5% for each transaction (depending on the card company) for getting his money immediately! So every sale he makes is reduced by 2.5% - 4.5% automatically! It's widely accepted and simply considered "cost of sales." The difference with the credit card company is that they also charge you, the user, an annual fee for the card plus extra charges when you don't cover your minimum balance in time. So, the credit card company takes actual fees from both ends! Yet, nobody has a problem with that, and hardly anyone ever claims that it's too expensive, because everybody (buyer and seller) realize sufficient benefits to make this transaction worthwhile.

7. I can see why you would calculate the discount that way. In fact, many people look at it that way in the beginning. But please allow me to demonstrate to you why this calculation is not quite correct. Let's say you had a $1,000 invoice in January and you received $700 from us in advance. Instead of paying you the remaining $300 when the invoice finally pays 30 days later, we deduct $50 and pay you $250 at the end. So, this is the 5% discount. Now, your concern was about the annual rate! So, let's say we do this not only in January, but each month for the rest of the year. In total, you will therefore have 12 x $1,000 invoices, i.e., a value of $12,000 per year. At the end of the year we will have deducted 12 times a discount of $50 on each invoice, i.e., a total of $600 per year. So, in a year, instead of receiving $12,000 from your sales, you only receive $11,400. But the $600 discount we deducted is still only 5% of the total $12,000 sales value – not 60% as you had originally thought.

If you find that people still maintain a "stubborn" view that 5% discount per month is equal to 60% interest per year, you're probably wasting your time with them. Move on! You will not be able to change their perception, and they're probably not really willing to listen anyway!

*"If all you have is a hammer,
you'll make every problem look like a nail."*

6.

The Art of Marketing and Advertising

Of course, good marketing is more than just having a good technique that you can use on the phone (or in fact, in any conversation with a suspect, a prospect or a customer). In a way – and although advertising is a part of marketing – marketing on the whole is a bit like advertising, as it shares the same objectives and follows very similar rules.

In essence, good advertising must accomplish three things. Let's agree that good advertising is advertising that is effective (i.e., it meets its objectives) and efficient (i.e., it meets its objectives quickly and at the lowest cost possible). So, what are the three key objectives of good advertising?

1. **It must create incremental awareness** of who **you** are and what it is **you** are offering

2. **It must have a relevant, differentiated, and credible message** for the target audience

3. **And it must ultimately persuade the target** to change their current behavior and buy the advertised product or service, or at least change their existing perceptions, attitudes, and beliefs in favor of that product or service.

Let's look at the role and importance of each of those three objectives.

Why do you want **incremental awareness**? Well, if advertising doesn't deliver any awareness on top of where you are right now, then why advertise? There are cheaper ways of addressing your existing audience. No, you advertise (and pay!) to generate growth and to become more prominent than you currently are.

Why do you need awareness in the first place? Isn't it enough, if they just hear your message and simply love it? Remember our radio or TV broadcast example? If your audience is not "tuned in" – in other words, is not aware of you – then how are they possibly going to get the message you are delivering?

Or worse, imagine they hear the message, love it, but don't know who it is from. You'd be advertising generically for the entire industry and might be driving your valuable prospects into open, competitive arms. So, **make sure you get your "branding" right!** Correct branding requires the message delivered and the benefit promised to be easily and unmistakably associated with you, your service, and your company and not to be confused with anybody else. For example: *"Ask not what your country can do for you. Ask what you can do for your country!"* is clearly associated with one person, and one person only.

The bottom line: You need the awareness as a platform, which enables you to better communicate with your target audience. Think of it as the box or podium on which you stand in front of other people. You're elevated, they see you better, because you stand out from the crowd, and it's much easier to listen to you than if you stood among the crowd in their middle. No platform, no communication. It's as simple as that.

Why do we need **a relevant, differentiated, and credible message**? Well, if one of the three is missing, guess what is going to happen. Right! Nothing!

If you're not relevant to your audience, they tune out. If you're not differentiated, they may as well deal with somebody else (and they probably will). And if you're not credible? How often do you deal with people you don't trust or don't believe a word they are saying?

The message (linked to the correct sender) is the key part of advertising, because it is the buyer's reason to buy. **While awareness generates attention, the message should contribute to retaining their attention and lead them to the buying process.**

For example, how often does it happen between spouses that one is talking to the other about something that is really important to him or her? He or she can go on forever, but if it's not relevant enough for the other one, and if it does not hold his or her attention, then after a while, all the other one hears is blah, blah, blah. Sound familiar? It's sad but true. Good marriage? Perhaps. Good communication? Definitely not.

Let's say you have done all the right things. You have the attention, you're able to hold it long enough to get the relevant message (and "branding") across, then why do **you need them to be persuaded to buy the product or service**? Well, if you pay for advertising, and it doesn't sell your product or your service, then what's the point? You spend time, effort, and money, yet you get nothing back in return. Does this sound like a sensible investment?

The same is true for marketing. **Whatever marketing you employ, there must be a measurable and incremental return**. And now we're getting to the bottom of it. Good Marketing must do all of the above, and most of all, it must provide an <u>incremental return</u>. Otherwise you are wasting your time and money.

But how do you know and measure whether or not your marketing is successful and delivers an incremental return? The next chapter provides the answer.

"Insanity is doing the same thing over and over, and expecting different results."

7.

The Marketing Plan: Your Way to El Dorado

In order to identify whether or not you are successful with your Marketing, you need a few things to begin with. First you need to define what success is. Then you need a plan and a monitoring system that tell you whether you're behind, on track, or ahead of your plan. Without these you will not know if you are successful. But how do you start?

1. You need to **set objectives and goals** that you want to achieve with your Marketing. These objectives must be measurable in units of time and return. They must have a clearly defined starting and ending point.

The best objectives are S.M.A.R.T. objectives because they are:

S_pecific
M_easurable
A_ction oriented
R_ealistic
T_ime sensitive

"I want to grow my revenue" is not a good objective. How do you know whether or when you are being successful? Are you successful if you only close one additional transaction in a year?

"I will grow my customer base from 10 to 20 within 5 months from today" is an excellent objective, because now you know where you're going, you can monitor progress, and you can take corrective action, if you see that you are off track. You also know that in order to generate 10 more clients in 5 months, you should probably generate 2 per month. In other words, you can break down your overall objective into "baby steps." For example, if you don't generate 2 new clients during the first month, you will have to generate 4 during the next month to stay on track.

2. But the objectives do not end there. Even if you generate 10 new clients in this period, what if each of them only completes one transaction? Is this the success you had in mind when you started this mission? Maybe, but maybe not. So, you have to expand your goal and be more specific. *"10 new clients within 5 months from today, generating a total of x dollars in incremental revenue."* Much better, because it's more precise. And again, if you see that one or two are lagging behind in their contribution to your goal as you move forward, you know you need more from the others and you better start doing something about it to stay on track.

3. Are you done yet? No, because revenue is only one dimension you may want to address. What if you sold your

service way under price? You'd probably achieve your objectives easily, but at what cost to your business? So you probably also want to include specific profit related goals. *"10 new clients in 5 months with a total of x dollars in incremental revenue and a y% growth in profit"*. There you go! Well, almost…

4. Let's say you market more than one service, for example factoring, credit card sales financing, and equipment leasing. You probably want to remain in control of how you grow your business, not just by how much. So you may want to include specific objectives for those services you want to market, because this will also determine how much time, effort, money and marketing you need to put behind each of them. *"10 new clients in 5 months with a total of x dollars in incremental revenue and a y% growth in profit. 50% of these incremental x dollars in revenue and y% profit growth will come from factoring, 25% from credit card sales financing, and 25% from equipment leasing"*. By quantifying your objectives that way, you will automatically prioritize your marketing focus on where you want it to be. If everything else was equal, with the above example it becomes pretty obvious that you would spend twice as much of your marketing resources on factoring than on credit card sales financing and equipment leasing. The point is: planning the details will bring you focus that you may not get otherwise.

5. And talking marketing, aren't you forgetting something? But of course! Targeting! Who are these new clients that will deliver all this additional revenue, and where do they come from? In order to spend your marketing budget (time & money) wisely, you better decide who to spend it on. Are you going to go after the "low hanging fruit"? They may be easier to attract, but the competition may also be fierce. Are you going after those clients that your competitors don't cater to? The niche may be smaller, and why aren't your competitors after them? Too difficult? Are they an opportunity or a risk? You better have an answer to these

questions before you decide where you are going to focus your efforts. *"10 new clients in 5 months with a total of x dollars in incremental revenue and a y% growth in profit. 50% of these incremental x dollars in revenue and y% profit growth will come from factoring, 25% from credit card sales financing, and 25% from equipment leasing. 50% of the new clients will come from service industries (e.g. staffing agencies and/or private investigators), and 50% will come from manufacturing companies".* Again, by being more specific and by drilling down deeper you increase the level of focus in your business!

6. Now, don't forget: **Good business objectives and goals are not limited to generating incremental business only from new clients**. In fact, for more established companies, a major share of their revenue is coming from retaining and growing their existing customers. Think about how you get them to "buy" more of the same [service] from you by shortening their buying cycle (i.e., this is a "frequency" strategy, by which you increase their rate of purchase). For example, if one client sells 50% of his receivables right now once a month, can you demonstrate that selling 60% or 70% twice a month instead would deliver better business results for him? Alternatively, can you get him to "buy" additional and different services from you (i.e., can you increase their "weight of purchase")? For example, if one client already sells his receivables, can you demonstrate that he would be better off by also getting advances against his future credit card sales, or that financing the new equipment he needs through an equipment leasing program would be more beneficial for him than buying it?

However, this may not always be easy or even possible in our industry. Unless there are some real benefits, it's close to impossible and rather unethical to make a customer factor more invoices than he needs to, so a "frequency strategy" seems to make little sense.

But what about "weight"? Perhaps you have identified other areas in which your customer could use some help. Maybe he could benefit from a cost reduction program in his business. Maybe he has other assets than Accounts Receivable that he might want to utilize. Maybe he needs a business plan. Maybe he would benefit from an equipment lease or lease-back program. Maybe he holds a note that he might want to sell in full or in part.

The point here is that the better you know your prospects and customers, the more you will learn about their business and the easier it will be for you to identify other solutions you just might be able to help them with.

Whether a "weight" strategy will or will not work for you is up to you to decide based upon what you know about your clients. However:

A good plan and goal will always consider and balance these three different ways of growing your business:

- **Building "Penetration"** (generate additional business from new clients)
- **Building "Frequency"** (get current clients to buy the same service more often)
- **Building "Weight"** (get current clients to buy additional services)

In order to determine what's right for you and what the best balance is, you need to **analyze your specific situation and where you stand with your business**. If you are just getting started, it is pretty obvious, but if you are trying to grow an existing business, it is a little trickier to make the right decision. But remember: **building business with existing clients is typically less expensive because you save on marketing and don't have to start from scratch. Therefore it can be more efficient and more profitable.**

7. OK, let's say you've got your objectives straight. They are broken down into the individual components; they are specific, measurable, action-oriented, realistic, and time sensitive. Now you can – and should – **monitor progress as you move forward**.

   How do you move forward? You have defined **what** you are going to achieve, now you need to define **how** you are going to do it. You need a plan and a strategy that tell you how you are going to achieve your goals and what detailed tactics and tools you will use to get there. It also needs to tell you how much time and money you will be spending.

8. Like the goals and objectives, the **plan and strategy need to be s.m.a.r.t.** (specific, measurable, action-oriented, realistic, and time sensitive). They need to specify what actions you will take, when, and for how long. What tools will you use, and how much will each tool or activity cost (both in terms of time & money)?

9. The **cost** part – and again this refers to both time and money – **is probably one of the most important elements in your plan**. Every business, no matter how small or how big will work within the constraint of a budget. You don't have one yet? Establish it! There is always only so much money and time or capacity available. But define how much you have and are willing to spend before you start. Don't leave it up to chance, because if you do, chances are you will either over- or under-spend it. Neither is good, because the budget should always be in relation to the results you will commit to achieve.

   But you have **two ways of tackling** that. You either start out with a given budget that you are willing to invest or can afford to spend on marketing, and then develop your plan from there (based on what your available time and money can buy). Alternatively, you can start out by listing everything you would ideally want to do and allocate the appropriate time and money funds to it. Once you're done, you probably find that you want to do more and spend way more than you can realistically afford (in terms of both time and money).

For most of the businesses and marketing plans in which I was involved, I have always preferred the second option. It is definitely less likely to kill good ideas too early.

10. Now it's time for making adjustments. You either adjust the time and money you will spend on each activity, or you adjust the number and/or the types of activities, or you adjust the expected outcome, i.e., the results or your goals and objectives. Personally, I have never written or seen a good plan in my life that didn't need these types of adjustments.

However, be careful how you adjust your plan. Many people struggle with giving up anything they had earlier identified as something they definitely want to do. They rather stick with all the marketing tools they want to employ, and adjust the time and money they invest in each individual component. They end up doing a lot of different things, but due to time and budget restrictions, they end up doing none properly.

This is not a good approach. Everything you do needs focus and "critical mass", before it becomes effective. **If you have to juggle a time and monetary budget, go deep rather than broad in your marketing efforts.** Do fewer things, but do them right. It's not just what you do, it's how you do it.

For some reason, many small business owners and people who are self-employed often fear the planning process and frequently shy away from it. They see goal setting and planning as an endless pain and lot of work. They believe all they need to do is just go full speed ahead, give it their best shot, and the results will speak for themselves. The latter part is actually true by the way. Without goals and a plan, the results will definitely speak for themselves, but it may not be anything we'd like to hear.

Others shy away from planning because they have never done it before in their life. They believe they cannot possibly do it because they lack the experience and expertise to write a good plan. But trust me on this: If you follow the guidelines as outlined herein, and if you're not afraid of spending a little time to think about all the details in your business, then you can write as good a plan as anybody else. It is not about eloquence – you're not writing it for anyone but yourself – or 100% precision. It's only about understanding your business, being willing to sit down and think it through, and putting the puzzle pieces (the details) properly together to compose the "big picture". Although the big picture is where you want to end up, unfortunately successful business owners cannot take a short-cut, start there and forget all about the details. The details is where you live on a day-to-day basis, and without them, your big picture will look pretty distorted.

But believe it or not, **goal setting and planning are actually fun processes because they require a lot of flexibility, creativity, blue-sky thinking, and dreaming. They provide a lot of freedom to determine your own fate.** You start with big ideas, great goals, and a lot of "what ifs," and in the end, you come to a level of realism that will make you very comfortable.

The insurmountable heap of questions and threatening uncertainties are gone. It's your plan, your goals, and you will feel confident that you can achieve them. Best of all, you know exactly what you will have to do to get there.

Now, one word of caution and a caveat. Once you have a plan, don't stop thinking about your business or how you can improve it as you move forward. Contrary to good communication, a business or marketing plan is the right place for certain assumptions, as you can never predict every little detail up front. **There will be times on your way to success when you may need to deviate from your plan, because certain things in the market or in your personal or business situation may change.** If this is the case, be flexible and adapt.

Simply adjust your plan again according to the new realities. Don't make the mistake of thinking that you slavishly have to follow everything just because it's on paper. But equally, because you may have to adjust your plan, don't think that the original efforts in establishing one were wasted. Just remember:

A good business and marketing plan is to a company what a map, a compass, and the stars are to a ship. Without them, you have no clue where you're going and how to get there. Your destination is uncertain, and chances are, you'll end up elsewhere.

Not a good strategy for running a successful business.

Practical Matters

8.
Marketing Versus Selling

As the ultimate goal and objective of marketing is to sell your products or services, one is often tempted to confuse marketing with selling, and therefore tends to use these terms interchangeably. Although the goal is the same, marketing and selling involve very distinct processes and tasks. Marketing activities and procedures prepare the process of selling. Selling – which has a lot to do with the right negotiation and closing techniques – is at the end of the marketing chain. In other words, it's a continuum on a time axis that looks somewhat like an overlapping bow tie:

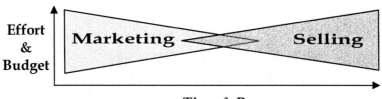

I'm not suggesting that marketing stops at one point, and that we focus only on selling from there on. Both are ongoing activities. But if we were looking at only one transaction or project, this is pretty much what it would look like. Marketing activities are important in so far that they put us in a position to sell. Without the marketing, how would we even get to an opportunity to sell?

By the way, as a small factor I don't think of what we do as "selling." Selling was what I did when working for corporate America. As a small factor and business consultant, I believe our real mission is helping people and companies become more successful and achieve their goals.

Ironically, as a small factor we are literally not even selling anything at all! On the contrary, we are buying our client's receivables. And as a consultant, you don't sell or buy anything either. You are simply helping your clients to grow their business. Yet, many people believe they constantly have to "sell themselves" or that "everything is selling."

This paradigm and way of thinking has become so much part of our culture and even found its way into our language, that we don't really think about it anymore and just accept it as a given.

"You have to sell your idea to the boss"; "He's not buying it."; "I'm not sold on this"; etc.

Good ideas don't have to be sold! They are presented and welcomed (or sometimes rejected for that matter). Bad ideas shouldn't be presented, let alone get accepted, and should certainly not be dressed up to "sell" them. And when someone is "not buying it," it simply says that this person didn't believe the message to be true or the idea to be good. Or you simply may not have presented it in a way that was convincing enough.

But this has absolutely nothing to do with "selling" and "buying" in the truest sense of the words. And this is where the boundaries between "selling" and "marketing" often become blurred and where many mistakes are made when it comes to our industry and factoring.

You should not – and cannot – "sell" factoring. Either it is a good idea or service for a business or it is not. Either there is a need for it or there is not. Either your prospect perceives it as a good idea or he does not.

Remember, marketing factoring is great. "Selling" factoring is not. But if you get your marketing right, then you won't even see a need to "sell" it.

9.
What Works or Doesn't Work (for Us)?

What marketing tools and activities have worked successfully for our business? There are a few, but to name the top three, they would be networking, networking, and networking. In exactly that order!

Networking

This is where we spend about 80% of our marketing time and budget. The reason we are so focused on networking is simple. It works. Networking allows us to do what I believe is paramount in our business. We meet new people every time, we are able to build better relationships with people we already know, and word spreads like wildfire and starts a "snowball effect". Even when the people we meet are not "hot prospects" for us, they often know someone who is. As the market becomes increasingly aware of our company and services, referrals come in from everywhere.

When we started out, our original plan was to focus on local businesses in Florida. Eight months later, we found ourselves with a client portfolio that spans from New York to California, with many states from north to south in between.

Of course, it also helps that factoring for small or midsize companies is still quite a novelty for many small business owners. So the element of positive surprise is on our side as well. A lot of what we do is also centered on education. Most small business owners are unaware of the opportunities that cash flow instruments – and specifically factoring – can provide. Once they understand, they are much more willing to listen and to give us leads or refer others to us.

The opportunities for networking are phenomenal. We are members of two of our regional Chambers of Commerce, the Better Business Bureau, the Financial Club, and various business networking groups in our area. We also work closely with a non-profit organization that provides business loans, and when they can't help their customers with a loan, they often refer them to us.

In addition, we have established a close relation with our local S.C.O.R.E Chapter (the Service Corps Of Retired Executives), who provide free consultation and can arrange SBA loans to entrepreneurs who want to start a business or are looking to expand their current operations. And if their clients do not qualify for an SBA loan, they now know where to send them!

One of the greatest benefits we get from this type of strategic networking is the snowball effect it has. And our cost is no more than some annual membership fees.

The BBB does not provide direct referrals but lists you in their directory, and people can obtain information about your company on line. This is not what I would consider classical networking, or recommend to all consultants, but I've heard from clients that they have actually "checked us out" through the BBB records before deciding to contact us.

Our clients are another great source of referrals. We are honored and find it very satisfying to see how eager our clients sometimes are to refer other people to us. Surprisingly, many of them don't even want the referral fee we offer for referring a new client to us. This suggests two things:

1. Those clients like <u>what</u> we do for them
2. They like <u>how</u> we do it

Customer Service

This is another marketing tool of utmost importance: **customer service**. Across most industries with highly fragmented and saturated markets the products or services often struggle to differentiate themselves from each other purely on objective "quality" criteria.

In factoring, these objective "quality" criteria would be the rational features like the size of the advance, the discount, the process and the timing for paying rebates, etc.

But if you think about it, the result or the benefit for the clients is typically the same. No matter which program or factor they choose, they improve their cash flow by getting money more quickly.

The costs of factoring to a client are generally very similar across the board, but they are often just "packaged" or marketed differently, depending on which factor you look at.

We have one client who went "price shopping" before making a decision. Although our discount rates are very fair and reasonable for a small factoring business, we encouraged him to look around. We told him there is nothing in this world that someone, somewhere will not offer at a lower price. We also suggested he might be looking for the wrong thing, since the lowest costs are not typically the best value. We cautioned him to watch for hidden fees and features easily discussed and promised, but when put to the test of a written contract, may not hold water very long. We also reminded him that integrity, a trusting relationship, and good service are often worth more than the lowest possible discount.

Although he conceptually agreed, he still went shopping. A few days later he called us, thanked us for meeting with him, and told us that he had found someone else with whom he wanted to factor. The discount was "significantly lower and the gentleman was also very nice." We congratulated him on his great find and wished him all the best and success.

Two weeks later he called again. He said, "Ralf, I can't believe how right you were. What looked like a gem from the outside was nothing but smoke and mirrors. When getting to the close, all of a sudden there was a minimum volume I needed to factor, the contract was termed, and they wanted to come and inspect my office and charge me for their travel and time. Now I understand what you meant. If your offer still stands, where can I sign?"

In the end, **price is really not a strong variable on which Small Factors can easily differentiate themselves** and stay in business for long. As in any other industry, if prices are so low that a company can no longer make sufficient profits to sustain its business, it will eventually disappear from the market. Alternatively, extremely low prices require extremely low cost, and when companies start cutting costs below a reasonable level just to offer low prices, they often start sacrificing quality and/or service at the same time. In reality, many "low cost" offers are often just packaged differently, and the true costs to the client are simply just not as visible at first glance. However, lowest cost options are often not in the client's best interest, because they are not always the best value. (Of course, this does not apply to comparisons between high vs. low factoring volumes. High volumes carry lower discount rates than small ones. That's perfectly normal.)

However, when comparing like with like, many factoring prospects often "forget" that low cost is not necessarily best value. Instinctively – but also because they are often not very familiar with factoring and therefore don't know what to look and ask for – they will ask very quickly how much factoring will cost them.

Never fall into this trap, and never make the mistake of quoting a price too early, before you had a chance to build their value perception.

Chances are that you will not even be able to quote a good price, unless you or someone else had already analyzed the client's specific situation. Don't even quote a price range, because later on, all they will remember is the low end of the range you quoted. If the final quote is higher than that – which it is more often than not – they will be disappointed and probably trust you and the offer less, simply because their expectations have not been managed properly.

Don't evade the price question, but firmly explain instead that you cannot possibly quote a price without having analyzed the details. It's like going into a car dealership and asking the sales person how much a car will cost you. Before being able to quote a price, the sales person will first need to know what kind of car, what engine, what extras you will want. Establishing the costs of factoring is no different.

A good way of dealing with this pressure for a premature quote – from a marketing perspective – is to give an example like the car purchase, but relating it to your prospect's industry. For example, if your prospect is an electrician, you can demonstrate it to him by saying *"Imagine someone calls you up and tells you that all the lights are out and none of the AC outlets is working anymore. He wants you to fix it but wants to know what it costs. Would you not first need to understand whether you just need to put in a new fuse or rewire the whole house? And even once you determined that you'll have to rewire the whole house, wouldn't you need to look at the house first before you could quote a price?"*

So, if it is not the price that differentiates the various small factors, how do clients choose one factor over another? If they can get money from other factors at slightly lower or very similar conditions, why do they still feel more comfortable working with one and not another? What are or should they be really looking for? Three things:

- Integrity
- A trusting relationship
- Service excellence

In fact, these are actually three important cornerstones for any type of business. If you can provide them, you already have a very strong marketing tool. Use them constantly without any deviation, and you will boost your image and reputation in your market and in your industry, earn respect and trust from everybody with whom you work, and turn on a flow of constant referrals that will come your way. And your customer retention rate will be high.

We all know what constitutes integrity, and we all have our own personal ways of creating strong relationships. However, here are a few ideas that strongly signal "Service Excellence" in my book:

1. **Manage expectations**. Say what you do, and do what you say (on or ahead of time and in full).

2. **Take responsibility and be accountable** for everything you promise and deliver.

3. **If you err, try to err on the side of conservatism**. With anything you promise or do, it's better to under-promise and over-deliver than vice versa.

4. **Rise above the "norm."** Aim for customer delight, not just customer satisfaction. Satisfaction is what everybody else aims for. Since that has become the norm, it's not sufficient anymore for you to stand out and gain a competitive edge.

5. **Avoid "nasty" surprises.** No business likes surprises (unless they're positive). Typically, people in business look for reliability. They like to be able to predict things. If you're unpredictable, you're a loose cannon.

6. **Be proactive.** Don't wait until something has happened and react. Instead, make it happen if you can – or prevent it from happening if that is the desired result. Prevention is always better than cure.

7. **Go out of your way for your clients and prospects**, whenever you can achieve something that is important to them.

8. **Don't give up too easily** when you are trying to achieve something for your clients or prospects.

9. **Be a respected partner** to your clients and prospects. Listen to them and provide your honest opinion. Many people believe the client is always right. I don't. Sometimes they're really wrong, but if nobody tells them, they might make costly mistakes. If you can help prevent your client from making a mistake, it is always better to call things as you see them, instead of always agreeing, just because it's a client.

    Some people feel they can't be that straight with clients, because they put their clients on a pedestal. The truth is, clients are regular people who make mistakes just like you and I. Treat them like friends and always tell them the truth, even if you think they may not like to hear it. It might not be for everybody, but I could not do business any other way. In short, learn to say "no" if "no" is the right answer. You'll become a much more respected partner, and you will provide a much better service in the long run.

10. Last but not least – and this is of utmost importance – **always put yourself in their shoes**. See and evaluate everything from their perspective, not yours. Ask yourself *"What would I want, if I were in his/her position?"*

    Always put the client's goals and objectives ahead of yours. If you focus on achieving the client's objectives, you will find that you will achieve yours as well. It doesn't work the other way around.

    Remember, **"sales follow service."** Not only do your clients deserve great service right from the start, but you will also have one of the most relevant and important points of differentiation versus many of your competitors. So make it as easy and desirable as possible for your prospects and clients to work with you.

If you adopt any or all of these suggestions, you will soon have a much stronger marketing impact than you have ever had before. Yet, it comes at almost no additional cost to you. Often it's just a little shift in attitude and/or behavior that makes all the difference.

Business Cards

Of course, we use other marketing tools of a much more mundane nature as well. Nice looking, professional business cards are a must. Remember too, you never get a second chance to make a first impression. So, you definitely want to make sure that your business cards reflect who you are, what you stand for, and what you do. **Ideally, your business card stands out in a positive way from the gazillion other business cards that your prospects receive.**

Decent business cards that can do the trick – if you are somewhat creatively inclined – are available through VistaPrint online at very reasonable cost. You can even get them for free, if you accept a VistaPrint signature on the backside. It's not recommendable though. Your business cards are your signature. Why run free advertising for someone else? The backside is actually a nice place to put a short message about your business. Again, a good opportunity to focus your message on client benefits!

Web Site

The other marketing tool that has become a "must have" is a professional web site. No matter whether you are a factor or a consultant, the web site is your most public face to the outside world. It is another key opportunity to set you apart from the crowd. In this day and age, you simply have to have a web site, if you want your customers and prospects to take you seriously.

Contrary to some other companies, our web site is more of an informational tool than a new business development device. We typically use our web site to direct potential customers to our services, **after** we have had an initial personal contact with them.

In this way, our site is a virtual brochure. In the past, people would typically ask for literature before they would even talk or meet with you. Nowadays you can direct them to your web site which does the same trick and much more.

And you really don't have to pay a lot to get a great site. We use Factor Solutions Inc.'s SiteBlu, the web site component of the BluBeagle^{TM} modular software suite, which provides highly professional web sites at very affordable prices starting at $250.

There are a lot of debates about what a web site should and can do for your business. Most people will agree that it is important to have your own web site, but when it comes to expectations as to what the web site should do for your business and how to achieve this, there is a rather large chasm between the different opinions.

Here are a few thoughts that may be helpful when making decisions about your web site and how to use it for your marketing purposes.

First, a comment that some of you may find very controversial, but which actually reflects valuable learning from corporate America: major studies for Fortune 500 companies have analyzed the effects of "interactive advertising" (web sites). They have proven that sheer "hits" and click-through" are not a good indicator for success. Contrary to the all too common belief that it's only a numbers game, efficiency and effectiveness of your web site are really not all about quantity, but quality.

What web site advertising and traditional advertising have in common is the need to convey a relevant, credible message for the "right" audience in an easily digestible format and presentation. There is also the strong need for a clear "call to action" and user-friendly navigation.

However, we know today that printed or on-screen material is never a replacement for the personal contact and the necessary rapport and relationship building process that is key to the conversion process from "interested prospects" into actual customers in our industry. It is rather an addition.

Hence, we don't expect to generate new business through our web site, but rather offer it as a quick information tool to prospective clients or consultants who are interested in working with us.

Therefore, we don't spend any money on getting better search engine results, because we know that it's not just about quantity. This learning has also been supported by the experiences that several consultants have shared with me. One of them reported that he gets 500 hits per day; however, these hits had not produced any tangible business results! And this is not an isolated case. I have heard very similar reports from many different people.

So when you think web site marketing is the only tool you need, and all the business will come your way, think again. If you only rely on your web site to do the job of prospecting for you, you can be sure that your success in this industry will remain a long way behind your real potential.

What should your web site look and feel like?

Well, obviously taste and individual preferences vary, but here are a few thoughts and suggestions you could consider:

1. In terms of design, I recommend you choose colors and images that look serious and professional and are appropriate for your business, its positioning, and our industry. Don't go color crazy, or else your site will look like a picture of an M&M contest.
2. Think carefully about the page layout. If the pages are overloaded with too much text, and the text layout is a bit

hard on the eyes, it won't draw the eyes to the highlights and the most important sections, but rather make them wander around and not allow the reader to take it all in.

3. Try to avoid text that "flutters." Instead choose "justified" text, which is easier on the eyes.

4. Balance the amount of text with "white space." Give the eyes a break!

5. Don't make the font size of the text too big or too small, and don't use too many different ways of highlighting important text sections, (i.e., different text colors, underlining, bold print, italics, capitalization, etc.). Rather stick with one or two.

   By the way, caps are considered "shouting" on the net! Remember that your web site is a communication tool that – like a brochure – communicates with only one visitor at a time. Nobody likes to be shouted at. It also has this "pushy salesman" ring to it: "hey, buy me!" It's not a positive in our industry.

6. Another important aspect is focus: Don't go overboard on the number of links and pages. Too much of everything will create an uncertainty of where to go next. And after a short while, the eyes will get "tired" and one will stop reading. Instead, make it "inviting" for visitors to browse and easy for them to navigate. When visitors are not really sure where to look or where to go next, they will get lost, and chances are they will leave the site all together.

   Too many links to "other" services will also make people wonder what it is <u>you</u> do! If your site is not focused, you also run a risk of getting responses from people who have no idea what you do, and who are looking for something completely different. That's a real waste of time for them as well as for you!

7. And of course, think carefully about the most crucial part: the communication contents. Don't fall into the common trap of giving away too much detailed information about

your products and services and making a lot of "statements." This would result in a rather feature driven approach that doesn't close the loop to the way more important factual and emotional benefits for the reader. And if you already give away all your information on your web site, then what added value will your potential prospects get from contacting you?

If anything, you increase your chances of getting responses from people who have already exhausted all other options of obtaining financing. You become their last resort (why would they call you before? They already got all your information from the web site!), which will exponentially lower your odds of providing them with a good solution.

8. Like with any other form of communication, make sure your web site text is written from a customer perspective and that it is not all about you.

Here's an easy way to check whether communication is self-centered or "customer-focused": count the number of "we," "I," "my," "our," "this product/service" etc. in the text and compare it to the number of times you have used "you," "your" sentences. Feature driven and self-centered communication uses way more of the former, whereas benefit driven communication focuses much more on the latter.

Then, compare the number of statements you make to the number of questions you ask. Again, feature driven communication uses many general statements that typically lack personal relevance to the reader (the proverbial "shotgun" approach), whereas benefit driven communication is more about your target audience and uses more questions, thus making it more personally relevant to the individual reader.

For example, when addressing an individual, it is much more personal and relevant to talk about "you," "your business" than referring to "individuals" and "businesses" (which is much more general and less personable):

"We/these services/products deliver a better cash flow to individuals and businesses."

It may be all true; but is it really exciting to me? It doesn't point towards my problem, doesn't address me personally, and it doesn't make it obvious that you are the best solution.

You can easily modify such statements into questions, personalize them, make me more curious, and entice me to contact you:

"Is your business slow or not living up to its full potential? If you are looking for a way to turn this around, you have come to the right place. At MyCo we specialize in helping you turn your mid- to long-term assets and receivables into immediate working capital for your business. Call us now to find out how. No strings attached!"

Or, *"Has your bank already said 'no' to your request for extra money for your business? If you would like to learn quickly how to turn a 'not now' into a 'here's how,' remember that we specialize in exactly this area and our advice is absolutely free. You have nothing to lose, except a good opportunity."*

These are just a few quick and rough examples of how communication can be made more personal and more relevant for the reader. Obviously, there are many different ways of achieving this goal, but that's the general idea.

Brochures

We also use brochures that summarize what we do and list the key benefits for a client, as well as a few selected client testimonials. When it comes to generating new business, brochures are not necessarily a power tool. They rather complement our marketing approach in terms of retaining attention, building relationships, credibility, and trust through education. They have a reminder function after the first meeting – and after we have already explained what it is we do, how we do it, and "what's in it for them." Like web sites or any other printed mass communications, brochures are not a substitute for verbal and personal contact and communication; they are merely an addendum, a visual stimulus, a reminder.

We frequently use our brochures as a visual aid and working paper during a meeting. When we leave it behind, we have often scribbled on it or highlighted the parts that are of particular relevance and importance to the person we met with. That is another way of "personalizing" mass communication material.

In order to have a more personal focus in our brochures, we have developed three different types: one for potential clients, one for bankers, and one for lawyers and CPAs. Whereas the body and core copy are pretty much the same throughout all of them, the benefit communication varies by target group. Why? Client needs and benefits are different from the benefits that a banker, a lawyer, or a CPA gets from referring customers to us. Cookie-cutter communication and marketing have died long time ago. One size definitely does not fit all.

Since we print our own brochures (in color and on special paper), and don't produce more than we need, we can constantly control our costs and inventory. We could have them done by professional printers as well at very similar costs, but we'd lose some of the flexibility of making changes as we go along, and we'd probably end up having to order more than we need to keep the per unit cost down. So far, we are happy with what we produce ourselves, and it certainly does the trick and meets our objectives.

Cold Calling

What about cold calling? We don't cold call on prospects, but we do cold call to establish contacts with potential referral sources, such as bankers, lawyers, and CPAs.

These people can be excellent catalysts for reaching a broad spectrum of potential prospects, which are almost pre-qualified already. However, lawyers and CPAs tend to be less valuable as referral sources than bankers. And among bankers, the ones from smaller banks and community banks tend to be more open to providing referrals than those at the larger banks.

For example, if the banker can't help someone find money for the business through their banking program, what is he or she going to do? Send them away, perhaps to another bank? No! Many bankers would much rather be part of the solution. If they can send their "rejects" to us, and if we can help them, everybody is a hero in the eyes of the clients, and everybody wins!

And for all of us cold-call-cowards out there, here is some more good news: Since we don't really "sell" anything to the banker, the cold call to them is no "threat" at all. All we're really doing is providing them an opportunity to "retain a future client." No cost or strings attached. It's more like offering a helping hand to a neighbor. There is nothing "threatening" about that.

In summary, our ongoing and constant marketing tools and activities include strategic networking, forming alliances, building relationships, educating potential clients and specific interest groups (e.g. bankers, lawyers, CPAs) who have a catalytic effect in generating referrals. We support all these activities with business cards, web site, and brochures.

The Icing On The Cake

Last but not least, our favorite and most productive networking and marketing team for our business is the group of consultants.

We have put together a comprehensive package and generous incentive program – at the top end of our industry – for consultants who work with us.

But almost more importantly, we spend a lot of time training and educating them on what they need to know to be more successful with their business. To the outside world, they represent themselves, they represent our industry, and they represent our company and services. Three excellent reasons, why we often go the extra mile to help them succeed!

When they are new to our industry or ask for help, we do everything we can to help them overcome the first hurdles or anxieties. We try to get to know them, we offer to accompany them to client meetings or participate in conference calls, and we provide them with the support they need to feel comfortable during client discussions and/or meetings.

As they are an important extension of our own marketing arm, it is of course important for us as well that the way they represent us in front of the clients is in line with our own positioning.

During my life within corporate America, I used to have a sign on my office door. When the door was closed, which was hardly ever the case, you would read: *"Please enter if you're my wife, my client, a new prospect, or my boss. Otherwise, please leave a message and I will get back to you."*

Now that we run our own business, I don't have that sign anymore. (Gee, I don't even have a door anymore, come to think of it.) But if I did, it would still include the same elusive group of people that I will always make time for, except "boss" would be replaced with "consultant."

Advertising

We have used **print advertising** sporadically in local dailies and weeklies, but not with any measurable or immediate success. Although our "ad test group" of clients, friends, and advertising experts at the papers confirmed that our ads were good, both in terms of visuals and copy, and we were using 4" x 6" sized ads, a decent size, advertising response and results were disappointing.

It might have been the wrong papers – but were all the other advertisers in there wasting their money, too? Personally, I believe the reason for non-response was our low advertising weight. We were just not in it long and frequently enough to reach critical mass.

You really need to stick with it for a while; but do the math. As a small factor or consultant, many businesses will not have the budget and stamina to do this kind of advertising long and frequently enough to see direct sales effects. Again, remember there are always the exceptions to the rule…you might just get lucky and receive an immediate response.

The bottom line: we don't know what soft effect the ads had or how much they contributed to building our awareness and image in the market, but they have not generated any revenue or any new prospects.

And thinking about marketing tool efficiency, I will rather spend my marketing budget on other vehicles that I know have provided us with a better return.

In all fairness, there are some people who have reported good success with advertising. However, these are people who advertise more or less regularly or at least periodically and spend quite a bit of money behind it.

As we all know, advertising needs to reach a "critical mass" level before it becomes effective. But unless you're willing to spend up to "critical mass" or beyond, you might as well not even bother to start. And as long as I don't get access to free or very inexpensive advertising, it just does not fit my idea of a suitable marketing tool for the smaller budgets.

Direct Mail

Another unsuccessful marketing tool for us is also another mass approach: **direct mail**. We have used flyers that we distributed via placement at "strategic" locations, such as the Chamber of Commerce. We figured that this was an excellent way of focused targeting. Think about what type of people visit the Chamber of Commerce: typically business folks.

First, we made some very moderate and humble calculations to see if we could handle all the business that would come to us that way. We ran our numbers: maybe 10 visitors a day, that's 50 per week and 200 per month. Let's assume 150 of them actually noticed our flyers (remember, they were "strategically" placed!), but the majority of 90% would not even be interested. This should leave us with 15 interested people each month.

Let's assume we only convert 20% of those that are interested.... Wow, that's 3 new clients a month! Wait. What if we convert 40%? That's 6 new clients per month. We may need to start thinking about capacity management in no time. But what if we only convert one person to become a client? Not bad either, since the return would still justify the effort and cost (we printed the flyers ourselves, so they were not a high cost item).

Exciting? You bet! Long story short, we did not get a single client that way. Worse, nobody even called! Were all our assumption and calculations wrong? Was the flyer not visible enough? Was it not clear or interesting? Was it going to be one of those "delayed effects" again, like advertising? Or may be it was a combination of some or all of the above?

Fact is, we didn't get anything out of it, but we didn't really know the reason(s). At any rate, we were not impressed with the results, and we haven't used "non-qualified mass communication vehicles" again since. Well, almost.

One of the Chambers of Commerce of which we are members was promoting their own Chamber services and was planning to send a fax-flyer to all the 1,700 or so Chamber members. They had asked if we wanted to provide a flyer to promote our business that way.

This was a zero-cost promotion for us, since they only needed one original copy. We agreed and sent them our flyer. We received one response (0.06% of 1,700 or so flyers distributed) and zero clients. Besides the fact that such non-solicited fax promotions are being outlawed anyway, such a "direct mail" approach does not appear to be a very effective and efficient marketing tool for us.

But let's think about "direct mail" for a moment. Let's say you get one response out of 1,700 mailings, and you need at least two interested prospects to generate one client (i.e., we just assume an optimistic 50/50 chance of success).

With such a scenario, you would have to mail out 3,400 letters to get one client. Postage alone would amount to almost $1,260 at regular price, although you can get reduced postage costs for sending out bulk mail. If you also had to buy addresses to do this mailing, it could easily add another $300 or so. OK, you can save some money here by typing up 3,400 addresses from your Yellow Pages. But still! Just those simple out-of-pocket costs for generating clients that way don't seem to make this idea particularly attractive for a small business.

A very computer savvy consultant reported another interesting story: He wrote a computer program and had managed to download 300,000 addresses from the Internet.

He then sorted them and started his direct mail campaign. The whole process took about 12 days of his time, and his out-of-pocket costs were limited to postage.

He reported the following results: For each 1,000 mail shots he sent out, he got between 25 – 30 responses. Do the math! With 300,000 addresses, this would leave him with 7,500 – 9,000 responses of obviously interested prospects.

I was thrilled! I thought, gee, two weeks of work for collecting the addresses plus postage of a mere $69,000 for sending out 300,000 post cards will yield about 8,000 interested prospects. That's a per unit cost of about $8.63 for each interested prospect.

Wow! If I worked 8 hours a day and did nothing but follow-up and pre-qualify 8,000 interested prospects, this will keep me busy for a period of 500 working days, if I only need 30 minutes for each follow-up and pre-qualification.

If I can fund or successfully refer only one out of ten interested prospects, this will leave me with about 800 deals. Each of those has to give me an average return of about $86.30 to break even on my initial investment of $69,000 for postage. But then I would have still invested about 1.5 years of my time in follow-up and pre-qualification, not counting the additional time I would need to get them actually funded.

But maybe my initial conversion of "1 deal per 10 interested prospects" is too pessimistic, and my return will be even higher? So, I went back to the consultant and said: "OK, I understand you get 25 – 30 responses from interested prospects per 1,000 mail drops. This is great, but how many deals have you closed from those so far?"

To this he answered: "So far….. exactly zero." At that point my initial enthusiasm immediately dropped to exactly the same level.

He did explain though that the reason for not closing any of these opportunities was the fact that at the time he started this venture he was still rather inexperienced in our industry and that the funding sources had simply not come through on some of these deals.

Indeed, and in all fairness to direct mail, some other consultants have reported that they have had "some success" with this tool though. I don't know exactly how they define "some success", but obviously there must be a way to work the numbers so they make sense from an efficiency and financial perspective. I may simply not have discovered it yet.

But that is part of the beauty of Marketing. There are many tools, options, and possibilities available to all of us. In the end, everyone has to find and decide what works for him or her, and what doesn't.

In my mind, a better way of using direct mail would be to combine it with "cold calling." Instead of sending mass mailings, you could send very small and manageable batches of letters to selected business owners of smaller companies or to the decision makers in larger organizations.

But instead of waiting for them to contact you, write your letter in a personal style that addresses them, their company, and business sector personally, and let them know that <u>you</u> will be calling <u>them</u> shortly to ***"discuss the potential for a future cooperation regarding the opportunity to secure an open credit line for their business."*** But do not mention factoring or any other details. Alternatively, don't mention that you will be calling them, and just wait a few days before you call and follow up.

When you call, it's not even a real "cold call" anymore, because you already have your letter as the "ice breaker" to which you can refer. It is actually very similar to calling someone because of a referral. Not as powerful, of course, but the dynamics are very close.

Now, three things can happen: Either they kept your letter and remember it, or they didn't receive it (or threw it away), but will let you tell them what it was all about, or they are absolutely not interested and will tell you right away.

The first two options give you a real chance to explore further and potentially move forward. These are obviously your opportunities. The third alternative will be an efficient way of finding out early and quickly that you really don't need to spend any more time with this prospect and can move on.

By the way, some people don't even send a letter at all to save on postage, and during the "follow-up" call just say that they are calling in regard to the letter they sent. It's not something I would personally like to do, as I would feel uncomfortable trying to start a relationship with a "white lie." But the truth is it's likely to produce very similar results compared to actually sending a letter first, since most people don't keep or remember most letters anyway.

Now, the bottom line about all the marketing tools we have used and will or will not use again is very simple. Unqualified mass-marketing tools are not for us. We see more benefit in establishing direct personal contacts either ourselves, through our consultants, or though other third party referrals. We simply achieve a higher level of effectiveness and efficiency with those tools and approaches.

The next chapter explains in more detail why efficiency in particular is such an important dimension and what you can do to improve or maximize the efficiency of your daily work.

10.
Marketing Time and Budget

As I consider everything we do that has a "visible" or "audible" impact on the outside world to be "marketing," it is somewhat difficult to say how much we really spend on marketing. Likewise, it is even more difficult to suggest how much you should spend on marketing your business. It will depend on how much time you can invest and how much money you can afford or are willing to spend.

For us, the time part of the equation is relatively easy: Marketing – according to my definition – accounts for about 80% of our time. But what value are we putting on our time? My best guess: probably not enough!

In terms of out-of pocket cost for marketing, we budget low. And it seems only prudent and common sense to recommend that as well to everyone else.

Particularly when you're relatively new in the industry, you don't want to go totally marketing crazy and spend a lot of dollars before you actually make some. It's much wiser to start low and grow in a controlled and managed fashion over time than hitting the market with a bang.

Even today, our own out-of-pocket marketing costs are limited to business cards, brochures, and membership fees that don't break the bank. But we do keep a separate budget for extraordinary items, such as travel and subsistence for public speaking engagements, meetings, and conventions or prospect and client entertainment.

When we started our business, we sat down and wrote a marketing plan. Why? Because it is a time-proven fact that:

"A good business and marketing plan is to a company what a map, a compass, and the stars are to a ship…."

Obviously, we had no idea which activity or marketing tool would generate success. So we made assumptions. We decided we wanted to be members of the aforementioned organizations and use their meetings for networking purposes. This would give us a fairly good indication of how many contacts would lead to how many leads, which in turn would lead to how many clients and projects.

Outside of these networking groups and meetings, we want to talk and meet with x number of banks, y number of lawyers, and z number of CPAs per month. (Note: x, y, and z will vary and are determined by your resources and capacity, i.e., how many hours you can dedicate to such activities). We then break these numbers down into weeks and days. This becomes our "to do" list for the day-to-day business.

Once you have these numbers down, it is relatively easy to assign the appropriate dollar amounts to each in order to see what your out-of-pocket costs will be to achieve the goal in the plan.

We then monitor our actual performance against these targets, so we can see if we're on track, behind or ahead of schedule in order to take corrective action, if necessary. For example, if we want to talk with five bankers per week, and we only manage to see three of them this week, well, we know our target for the following week will be seven.

To stay on track with our plan and to make sure we meet our business goals, we also do what I call **"reverse planning."**

This is how it works. Let's say we know that on average, we get one client from talking with ten pre-qualified and serious leads, and the average client contributes $1,000 in revenue per month.

If we want to generate $10,000 in revenue per month, we need ten average clients. This means we have to talk with 100 pre-qualified, serious leads per month. How many serious leads you will have depends on how many contacts you make. How many contacts you make will dictate how many hours you need to invest, if you assume that one contact takes about 0.5 hours on average. And so on.

You can plan your entire business that way. When you do this, you will soon see what your potential earnings can be as a function of what resources (hours & dollars) you invest.

This is a great way of business and marketing planning. It allows you to monitor your progress and adjust your plan as you move forward, based on the results that you target and those you actually achieve.

Knowing how much time and money you invest and what return you are getting is priceless. It's in fact the only way to stay on top of your business and manage it in a forward thinking fashion.

11.
Does Size Matter?

Are successful marketing methods for factoring smaller clients different from those for larger clients? No, not necessarily. The tool kit available to any marketer is pretty much the same. Where they differ is in scale and scope.

Marketing, like many other things in business is also driven by budget. If you're a large factor, working with larger clients and dollar volumes, you have more money available for marketing. You can more easily afford to spend your marketing dollars on advertising, PR events, promotions, etc. You can afford to hire an ad agency, have dedicated business development people on staff, and so on. It is simply a function of the size of the league in which you are playing.

But how can so many small businesses coexist and be successful with these large players next to them? Simply because big is not always better. And needs and requirements of large companies are not necessarily the same as those of smaller players.

What large companies gain in "muscle" (scale and scope), they often lose in terms of flexibility, creativity, and service. Processes, procedures, and policies frequently replace individual interactions and personal creativity or decisions. Their size simply doesn't allow them to easily keep that personal touch or to be that nimble on their feet. They get the business done, but it's less of a "personal experience" and more of a "process." And you simply can't expect to have someone on the phone for you all the time or get a call back within two hours.

Often, this is not the fault of the individual people who work there though. Larger companies – and their employees – are under a totally different pressure system than any small company. Performance is mainly measured in hard numbers, and in order to improve results, larger companies are much more prone to restructuring, re-engineering, or whatever else one wants to call the process by which they are trying to become the "leanest machine possible." Typically, this puts more pressure on fewer employees, and now it is clear why the people can't always function as if they were running a boutique shop.

It's like buying clothes off a rack at Costco versus buying them in a small boutique with a lot of personal service. The boutique folks typically have the time and capacity to care.

I used to buy a lot of stuff in a particular boutique in Paris (no, not Texas). A couple of years after we had left Paris, I lost a special button on a jacket I had bought there. I sent them an email, explaining what happened. Two weeks later, I received a box in the mail. They had mailed me five extra buttons, just in case. To this day – although we haven't lived in Paris for years – I'm still on the mailing list of this particular boutique, and they never fail to send me a nice, personal note informing me about their new arrivals. And I usually end up ordering a piece or two. What a great way to retain customer loyalty! This is exactly the benefit that small factors and consultants can leverage in their business and marketing as well: flexibility, speed, service, and the personal touch.

A difference between marketing to smaller clients versus larger clients is in the communication and the packaging of the message itself. Large client companies have a different structure and hierarchy than small shops. The decision process typically takes longer and involves more people. A qualified

CFO of a large company is also likely to ask different questions than a small business owner.

Big companies are far more likely to know already what factoring is and how it works; smaller businesses typically do not. Hence, the former may have more of a need to discuss the rationale and your competitive (financial) advantage over other providers, whereas the latter will need more education and emotional reassurance. Therefore, larger clients will require a different communication focus of your marketing message than smaller ones, although the tools and methods to reach them are essentially the same.

However, the larger the organization, and the "higher up" your contact is in that organization, the less time he or she will have typically available to deal with you. Your approach and communication need to be more concise and to the point, and you should only expect to get some limited time to hold their attention and build that important relationship.

You may get away with a two hour working lunch with a smaller client, but you may have to make do with a 45 minute breakfast meeting with the CFO of a large organization, if you're lucky. Most of the time you'll probably end up in a half-hour business meeting in his or her office. And that is an achievement!

Elephants, Rabbits, and Quails

Another area where size really matters is when it comes to the tactical definition of your revenue target. Let's say you are a consultant who specializes in factoring, or at least you offer factoring as part of your portfolio.

Of course, at some point you are wondering how much income this business will generate for you. So, let's further say that you have decided to refer two million dollars in factoring volume to the funding source(s) each year.

How you maximize your income will largely depend on the mix of business, and to which factor(s) you take it. And this is where the elephants and rabbits come in.

Generally, high volume (big) clients will generate high $ income for the factor, but sometimes lower commission percentages for a consultant. And some bigger factoring companies often only pay the commission for a limited amount of time, typically only for the first year or for the first period of a termed contract with the client. Others pay commissions for life.

Small factors tend to pay higher commission percentages to the consultant and typically for the life of the account. But since the overall factored volume is lower, absolute commission dollars are obviously less per deal.

Here is an example that illustrates how it works:

If you only find one 2-million-dollar-per-year client (that's your "elephant" with about a $167K factoring volume per month) and set him up with a larger factoring company, you may make about $9,000 per year (or roughly $750 per month).

This is based on the factoring company collecting 3% for 30-day invoices. So they would earn $5,010 per month. Even if they paid you a 15% commission of their fees (typically commissions are between 10% and 15%), that would compute to roughly $750 per month or $9,000 per year for you.

However, if you instead find ten $200K-per-year clients (these are your ten "rabbits" who factor about $16.7K per month each) and place them with one or more small factors, you probably make about $125 for each of them per month, which computes to a total of $1,250 per month or $15,000 per year.

This assumes that each $16.7K monthly invoice volume earns 5% for 30 days, which computes to $835 per month for the factor. With the same 15% commission for you, there's your $125 commission check for each invoice right there! And since you have 10 of those "rabbits," that's your $1,250 commission check per month, or $15,000 per year.

Neither one of the two scenarios provides you with an income to live on for a year, but it's still a pretty impressive difference.

And it gets better with time: small factors will typically pay your commission for the life of the account. So even if none of these 10 "rabbits" will grow their factoring volume at all, and just continue what they're doing now, you'd be looking at $15,000 each year, only for having brought these 10 clients to one or more small factor(s) once!

It may not buy you the million-dollar-home, but it can easily put a couple of nice new cars in your garage! Or if nothing else, it's simply just a very nice residual income.

Now, why does it work like this? The reason is simple: smaller factoring volumes have higher discounts, whereas larger volumes command lower discounts. Many consultants don't realize how much more profitable it is for them to focus on smaller accounts! It's often too easy to fall into the trap of only seeing the big commission numbers from big factoring volumes!

Hence, many people only chase the "elephants" (which are much smaller in numbers and much harder to hunt) instead of the "rabbits" (of which there are plenty, and they're much easier to catch!).

When you look at the two scenarios above, in both cases you have referred $2 million per year worth of business, but it's evident, which is more profitable for you! Yes, you'd have to find ten rabbits compared to only one elephant. But in fact, chances are you will find and catch them a lot more easily. And if one of them drops out over time, you still have nine others. But if you lose your income from this one elephant, you're out of money all at once. In other words, the risk to your business is much higher.

Now, if rabbits aren't your game, let's try it again, only smaller. Let's start with quails! Let's say your average "quail" factors only $10K per month. Assume the same 5% discount and your 15% commission. That's $75 per month or $900 per year for you in commissions for each "quail." With ten such clients your annual commissions add up to $9,000.

However, here is what usually happens: Clients grow past $10K to $20K, $30K and beyond. Let's stay true to life and say you have 10 clients who over time end up factoring this much:

- 4 factor $10K per month
- 3 factor $15K per month
- 2 factor $25K per month
- 1 factors $30K per month.

With the same 5% discount and your 15% commission, this is what your commissions look like on aggregate:

# of clients & volume	$ Volume per Month	Your Commission $		
		Per Client per Month	Total per Month	Total per Year
4 x 10,000	40,000	75.00	300.00	3,600.00
3 x 15,000	45,000	112.50	337.50	4,050.00
2 x 25,000	50,000	187.50	375.00	4,500.00
1 x 30,000	30,000	225.00	225.00	2,700.00
Total	165,000		1,237.50	14,850.00

Now, here's the kicker: factor two $5K per month clients yourself, in addition to referring everything else. With 5% discount, that's another $500 income per month or $6,000 per year for you.

Your income has just increased to roughly $21,000. Still not enough to live on, but you get the idea. Once you start buying a few receivables yourself, you'll probably want to refer less and less. You may end up wanting to factor full time and just refer deals that are too big for you to start with, or those which outgrow you (the latter of which are the easiest to place with larger factors).

The whole point about elephants, rabbits, and quails is that you can easily create your own roadmap to success by playing the numbers in a strategic way and by using the right tactics to support them.

You decide which income level you want to achieve and how to get there most efficiently. Big may be beautiful, but it's not always the best or most effective and efficient way to reach your goal.

Use the elephants, rabbits, and quails as a guide to determine your own strategy and for planning your income that way. They can also help you define your core target market and ideal client profile much better.

Once you know exactly what type and size of clients you're looking for in the market, you will actually find it much easier to find them. You will experience a very different level of focus, which will bring you closer to your goal so much faster.

12.

Presentations

Although we have a "standard" PowerPoint presentation about who we are, what we do, how factoring works, and what benefits for the business and the owner it entails, we take great care not to use it blindly on all occasions, particularly when we meet or talk with new prospects for the first time.

When we use it at all, we always make sure that we have sufficient information on the prospect beforehand, so we are always in a position to customize the presentation to the particular industry, business, situation, and personal interest and challenges. We use examples or similar cases relevant to them that they can understand and relate to more easily. We use number examples to which they can relate and that make sense for their individual situation.

For example, if their average invoice is $1,000, we demonstrate advances, discount, and rebates based on a $1,000 invoice. If their company is bigger, we may use a $10,000 or $100,000 invoice as the example.

If their reason for factoring is "survival," we emphasize benefits such as being able to pay taxes/payroll on time, whereas when they're in a "growth mode," we talk more about being able to accept larger orders, increasing inventory, hiring the extra sales person, and so on.

When talking to a financial expert in the company, we talk about time value of money, increased return-on-investment, no-debt and off-balance sheet financing, and the increase of net worth with the reduction in A/R investments, etc.

When addressing a small business owner, we show him how factoring can help with more efficient time management and the ability to focus on his business, his customers, and what he does best, as opposed to chasing invoices and completing administrative chores.

These are all ways we customize our communication to our audience. And this is really only for the 20% of the time that we do the talking. During the remaining 80% of the conversation – particularly during the first contact – we don't even want to go there at all. We much prefer to gather as much information about them, their company, their situation, and their "financial pain" as we possibly can.

We ask to see their P&L to be in a better position to understand where and when they are making how much money, how much they spend, and where it's going. We look at their Balance Sheet to see if factoring makes sense for them in the first place, or if maybe another asset based lending scenario would be more appropriate. Sometimes it even transpires that they don't really need factoring or any other form of financing at all, and all they really need to do is get their house in order. But that's fine!

Once we can determine that they really need some sort of financial injection, we typically explore different ways of business financing together with them first, before even going into factoring. The point is that we do not want to "sell" factoring per se.

Sometimes, people tend to make every problem look like a nail, because the only tool they have is a hammer! We believe that's not the right approach, because the client's needs must always come first. And no two clients are alike! If there's a better financing solution than factoring available to them, we want our clients and prospects to benefit from it and make it available to them, if we can. Remember too, what we do is not for everybody, and a "No" to factoring is perfectly OK.

"If we were all thinking and doing the same, most of us would be superfluous."

13.

Recommendations

Occasionally I get questions from new consultants as to how they should prospect for new clients. This is one of the most difficult questions to answer, because I believe **there is no cookie-cutter answer that is right for everybody.**

The answer really depends on what type of person you are, what your situation and background are, how much time and money you want to invest, and what opportunities you want to pursue.

I know what works for our business and for us as individuals, but it may not be the same for everybody else. I have referred to the most common marketing tools available to all of us.

Other, more individually opportunistic ones I have left out on purpose, in order to keep more focus. Although excellent in nature and cost neutral, not everyone can write articles and get them published or get frequent press releases about their business and services into the paper. But if you are one of those individuals who can, by all means, jump at every opportunity you get.

I'm sure there are even a good number of other very creative marketing opportunities that other professionals in our industry have come up with and used for their own business. Which of them, or which combination is most suitable and beneficial for each individual, I cannot determine. And I'm always a bit wary of those people who claim they can. **Each and every factor and consultant must eventually determine what works best for him or her.**

Choose your marketing tools according to your personality and your capabilities. For example, if you have never trained for public speaking or are terrified by the sheer thought of it, get trained first before deciding to use this vehicle. We love public speaking, make speaking opportunities happen, and jump on every one we get because we see positive results from it; but public speaking is not for everybody.

Remember too, successful marketing is not only about **what** you do, but also to a large extent about **how** you do it. For example, if you're not good at public speaking but still do it, you might find the results are not as positive as you had hoped. Is it therefore fair to conclude that public speaking is not a good marketing tool? Of course not! All you can say is that public speaking does not work for you!

Let's say you find ten who people claim they had no success with public speaking at all. Can you therefore conclude that public speaking doesn't work? Not necessarily, unless you know that all ten of them are excellent speakers and they only spoke in front of the "right" audiences.

The opposite is true as well, by the way. If ten people report that public speaking worked like a charm, it's not a guaranteed home run for you by definition. It's not all about **what** you do, but rather **how** you do it!

I have just used public speaking here as an example and for illustrative purposes. But the same applies to any other marketing tool as well. What works for some might not work for others. And what works for them may not work for you. And vice versa.

The one thing that will work for you and everyone else though is to write a good business and marketing plan, monitor over time how you progress, and make appropriate adjustments as you move forward. This will give you a clear roadmap and sufficient documented personal experience to decide what's right for you and what isn't.

One thing I will also say with full conviction and from the bottom of my heart: **keep your costs down, particularly when you're new to the game!** Don't fall prey to people or companies promising you fantastic results while all you have to do is pay them a lot of money for the product or service they're offering – no matter what it is or how easy, attractive, or credible it may sound. Some may be a real deal, but others are not. The problem is you won't be able to tell before you pay.

I know from my own experience and from that of others that **you do not need to make a high monetary investment to become a successful consultant or small factor**. Likewise, I know too many people – unfortunately many of them are newcomers – who have invested relatively large sums of money in all sorts of different marketing tools, which some "experts" had said were indispensable. The bottom line: they either got no or only very insignificant results, yet had invested everything they had available.

Marketing tools that cost a lot of money are often not the "Holy Grail" for small factors or consultants. If you decide to buy *anything*, get advice from someone neutral who has had experience with what you want to buy (tip: the seller or his agent are never the best source). Find more than one person who is impartial and who has had success with the tool in which you want to invest. And make sure their definitions of success are close to yours. But do ask more than one person. One person is *not* enough. *Ever!*

Another safe recommendation is to **make sure you're comfortable with your focus. You will need to be able to talk about it with passion and sufficient knowledge.** Start with a niche or an industry that you know something about, and make sure you know your "stuff" before going live with prospects. One way of doing this is with "dry runs." Role-play with friends and family; I know it sounds like a dumb game, but it will help you. Let them take the role of a prospect, and simulate different real life approaches. Then reverse the roles, so you get to play prospect. Remember: try to see everything from your prospect's perspective.

Also, **practice your listening and empathy skills**. Ask a lot of questions during your interactions with your prospects. Don't volunteer information that you have not identified as being of relevance and interest to them.

Before you decide to buy anything, try networking. And always ask for referrals. *Always!* Join networking groups in your area. You can find them through your local Chamber of Commerce or the S.C.O.R.E. Chapter.

One tip here: networking groups are easy and fun, but there are a few golden rules. Networking is not a sales opportunity, so don't try to sell. Get to know the people and their businesses, so you can also send referrals their way. It's always a two-way street. Meet as many people as you can, but ask about what they do. Don't run around trying to spill all the news about you; that will scare them away. People in these groups know how to play by the unwritten rules, so your turn will come when they ask what you do. But don't use it as an opportunity to talk about yourself and how great your services are. **Tell them what you do by telling them what's in it for the clients who work with you!** Remember too, everyone there is there for one purpose: improving business (theirs!).

If you decide to buy "leads" make sure they are pre-qualified for the purpose you want them. If they are just addresses, you might as well consult your local yellow pages. It has the same effect and is cheaper.

Don't believe that you can sit back and do everything on paper or online (flyers, direct mail, web site, etc.). Our industry is and will remain a people business. You need to build relations, credibility, and trust. You can only do this through personal contact. So get out there, mingle, and spread the word.

Closing

14.
Final Comments

I hope you have enjoyed reading this book and perhaps found one, two, or more nuggets that you can use to create your own magic and to produce this bigger bang with a smaller budget, by simply making your marketing more powerful, more efficient, and more effective at zero or low additional cost.

But even if you can only make one improvement to your marketing mix or the way you do business, or only close one deal more as a result of reading this book, it will already be a success.

From the bottom of my heart, I wish you good luck, lots of fun with all your endeavors, and tons of success in your business!

And if you ever feel you need some help, assistance, or clarification, or if you have any questions, comments, or ideas, please feel free to contact me by phone or e-mail anytime. I'd love to hear from you, and there are no strings or costs attached.

Sincerely,

Ralf Bieler

P.S.: If you think you could use some help with "selling," try Miller-Heiman's **free** e-tips on strategic selling. At www.millerheiman.com under "Publications," you can sign up for "Best Few" and "Free e-tips." Each month you'll receive a free e-zine with excellent tips & tricks on how to better manage the sales process and become more successful at selling and closing. The company also provides very good and professional sales training seminars, for which you have to pay. But since the message of this book is how to do great things on a small budget, you may want to stick with the "freebies" for a while.

Appendix

For Consultants

Sample Call Script for Small to Midsize Companies

You are: Patty Cash from MyCo
Your prospect: Seymour Green, owner of Lowondoe, Inc.

Good morning/afternoon/evening. I am Patty Cash from MyCo. I'm looking for Seymour Green.

Hi Seymour, I am Patty Cash at MyCo. We specialize in assisting small and mid-size companies like Lowondoe with their business financing. And as some of our funding partners are expanding their business, they are currently looking for more companies to fund.

As you would imagine, Seymour, our programs are obviously not for everyone, but Lowondoe might actually qualify for an open credit line that is interest-free and totally independent of your time in business, your own personal credit score, and the other criteria that your bank will typically require. Could such an open credit line possibly be of any benefit to Lowondoe?

<u>No</u>

1. How come?/Why is that?
2. OK, I perfectly understand that…….. (**REPEAT ANSWER**) right now.
3. Would it be OK for me to check back with you in the future, to see if things might have changed?
4. Of course, if you have any questions before then, you can always call me at 123-123-1234 or drop me a note via e-mail at Patty@MyCo.com
5. But Seymour, since I have you on the phone, do you know of any other business associates to whom you could possibly refer me, who might benefit from an open credit line for their business right now? We work with start-ups as well as with established businesses.

Thank and close

Yes

Is now a good time for you to talk for a few minutes Seymour, or would you prefer me to call you back later?

No, later

> 1. No problem. When would be a good time for you?
>
> 2. I'm sorry, Seymour, this day/time doesn't work for me. I'm actually with one of my clients at that time/on that day. Can we do it an hour/a day later?
>
> 3. Of course, if you have any questions before then, you can always call me at 123-123-1234 or drop me a note via e-mail at Patty@MyCo.com
>
> 4. By the way, Seymour, since I have you on the phone, do you know of any other business associates to whom you could possibly refer me, who might also be interested in an open credit line for their business right now? We work with start-ups as well as with established businesses.
>
> **Thank, confirm appointment, and close**

Yes

You see, Seymour, the funds that could become immediately available to your business through our program are only based on **your** sales. So, the more you can sell, the more money becomes available to you, and you never have to re-apply for a higher credit line. It grows automatically with your business. But of course, as with any other credit line, you only draw against it as much as you need and as often as you need. And you never pay any interest. Does this sound OK so far?

Yes

USE ONE OR MORE OF THESE BULLET POINT EXPLANATIONS SEQUENTIALLY, AND ONLY, IF NECESSARY. YOU CAN ALSO COME BACK TO THEM LATER.

- Would you like to hear how it works? When you bill your customers, through our program, we buy your invoices from you at a small, mutually agreed upon discount and pay you directly, right when you send the invoices. So you don't have to wait for your customers to pay you. Many clients tell us this is very beneficial to them, when their customers have 15 or 30 or more day terms (which they often don't stick to anyway). But no matter what terms **you** had to extend to your customers, you'll get most of the money (typically between 60% - 90%) up-front, and the rest – minus the agreed upon discount – when the invoices get paid.

- In fact, you can also think about it as being very similar to a normal credit card transaction, whereby the credit card company would charge you 2.5% - 5% (depending on the company) for each payment that one of your customers makes with a credit card. It's also very similar to offering your customers for example a 2% discount for paying their invoices within 10 days. With both of these scenarios, the intention and the effect is exactly the same as with our program: You get your money earlier, which is almost like turning your business into a C.O.D. operation.

- By the way, Seymour, you may or may not know this, but until relatively recently, this form of business financing was only available to very large corporations, who use it on an ongoing basis. It's about a multi-billion market! Small companies however, still had to ask their banker for a traditional loan or credit line (and we all know where that typically goes, right?).

- However, during the past few years we have seen that smaller companies – much like Lowondoe - can equally qualify for and benefit from this service. Hence, **we** focus all our efforts on helping these smaller and mid-size companies – like Lowondoe – to level the playing field a little and stay more competitive.

And this is why I wanted to talk with you today Seymour, to find out whether or not this is an opportunity for you and Lowondoe. Do you think – in principle – that you would benefit from having such an open credit line available to Lowondoe or not?

No

> 1. How come?/Why do you say that?
> 2. OK, I perfectly understand that ……. (**REPEAT ANSWER**) right now.
> 3. Would it be OK for me to check back with you in the future, to see if things might have changed?
> 4. Of course, if you have any questions before then, you can always call me at 123-123-1234 or drop me a note via e-mail at Patty@MyCo.com
> 5. But Seymour, since I have you on the phone, do you know of any other business associates to whom you could possibly refer me, who might be interested in an open credit line for their business right now? We work with start-ups as well as with established businesses.
>
> **Thank and close**

Yes

Well, Seymour, let's see then if we can qualify Lowondoe for our program. The quickest and easiest way for us to do this would be for me to ask you a few questions, and I'll write down your answers.

IF APPROPRIATE: AT THIS POINT YOU CAN ALSO SUGGEST A PERSONAL MEETING AND GO THROUGH THE PRE-QUALIFYING-PROFILE TOGETHER.

Alternatively, I could mail/fax/email you a very brief checklist that you can complete on your own time, and then mail/fax/email back to me. Which would you prefer?

Either way, we can tell you very quickly, if Lowondoe fits any of the standard programs or if we can customize a program for you that better fits your needs and requirements.

COMPLETE OR SEND PRE-QUAL-PROFILE.
DEFINE NEXT STEPS, THANK & CLOSE

For Consultants

Sample Letter to Prospects in Small to Midsize Companies

How much would <u>your</u> business benefit from an interest-free open credit line right now?

Dear … **(prospect's first name)**,

Having sufficient funds available at all times to run and grow your business profitably is a frequent challenge for many small and midsized companies like … **(prospect's company)** these days.

While many opportunities and options exist for multi-million dollar corporations to secure the business funding they need on an ongoing basis, financing for the smaller and middle tier companies still remains a scarce resource in our country.

No image is more daunting, and no sound is more disturbing across our nation than the slamming of a bank's door right in the entrepreneur's face, when he or she asks for financial help for their business.

As a result of all the restrictions and existing regulations by which traditional banks must operate, this may be understandable, but it is still very disappointing and frustrating. About 50% of our nation's Gross Domestic Product (GDP) is generated by exactly those smaller companies and entrepreneurs like yourself, who shoulder all the risks but have to carry the financial burden alone.

Just imagine where you, your business, and in fact, many other smaller companies – and thus our entire economy – would be, if only the right business capitalization was available to the smaller players, and if they were all more successful with their business ventures. In fact, 70% - 90% of companies fail in the market only due to under-capitalization. A rather scary perspective!

This is where we come in. At ….. **(MyCo)**, we have made it our single goal to help business owners of new and established small to midsize companies like you achieve their dreams and business objectives by providing quick access to creative financing programs outside the proverbial box that historically were only available to large corporations.

After all, what works for them, ultimately also works for the smaller business! All it really takes is just opening a door, adapting existing financing programs, and making them available to the small business community. And this is exactly what our funding partners have done very successfully.

No, we are not a new bank, and we don't perform miracles either. Of course, these programs are not for everyone. But chances are we may be in a position to provide you **access to an interest-free, open credit line for your business**. And as long as your customers are creditworthy companies or government agencies, you are not even required to have a stellar credit record or the typical 2-year business history. In fact, many clients are even start-up companies that would have never seen the light of day without this service!

As you can probably sense, we are obviously so excited about these programs and the great results they have achieved for companies like … **(prospect's company)** so far that I could easily go on and on about them right here. But since one size never fits all, I'd much rather talk with you to find out more about you and ... **(prospect's company)**, and whether or not this opportunity could be one for you.

So, if you can see your company benefiting from an interest-free, open credit line that automatically grows with your business, please let me know. We're here to help companies like ... **(prospect company)** level the financial playing field, and I would love to hear your thoughts about it.

You can reach me during normal business hours at ... **(your phone number)** or via email at **you@yourcompany.com**. There are no strings attached. And that's only my first promise to you!

Sincerely,

Your name
Your Title
Your Company

Here's what readers are saying about
Marketing Magic...

"The success of every business comes down to marketing. Whether your marketing budget is zero or a zillion, Ralf has put together an easy-to-read, solid book to help you succeed. Everyone should read this book...and probably more than once."

Fred Rewey
President, American Cash Flow Corporation
Author of *Winning the Cash Flow War*

A truly great read! You easily see why it is so important to really look at issues and challenges from a customer's perspective. And if we as marketing professionals don't strive to understand the things our prospects are either trying to fix, accomplish, or avoid, our efforts in creating sales opportunities simply become dilutive. The ideas presented in Marketing Magic are based on a sound methodology and help drive the effectiveness of marketing. Marketing Magic is marketing excellence at its best and recommended reading for all marketing professionals and those who just want to see more bang for their buck."

Jeff Brunings
Director, Marketing - Miller Heiman, Inc.,
Building Exceptional Sales Organizations

"Marketing Magic is an excellent presentation of typical and complex marketing problems and their solutions, which are deeply rooted in known marketing theory as well as in the author's profound and practical day-to-day experience. Both, problems and solutions are brilliantly adapted to the cash flow sector and provide the perfect background to understand its dynamics, while offering practical insights and clever tips that are worthy of being implemented in any factoring business. A great and very enjoyable read from which marketing novices and professionals alike can benefit tremendously."

Harald K Bellm, General Manager, Henkel Mexicana
A Brand Like a Friend

Here's what readers are saying about *Marketing Magic...*

"The benefit of *Marketing Magic* is the full perspective from a true expert in the industry as to how to market your business successfully with even the smallest budget. The author's many years of success in the business world, his expertise and unbridled enthusiasm for marketing, and his quick success in the cash flow industry, together make his insights and perspective both unique and highly valuable."
Jeff Callender, President, Dash Point Financial Services
Author of *The Small Factor Series* and *Marketing Tools for Small Factors and Consultants*

"Ralf's Marketing Magic is definitely recommended reading for all cash-flow professionals or those thinking about getting into the business. Everyone should have a well-used copy close to their desktop. Anyone involved in factoring or consulting will benefit immensely from absorbing and practicing the ideas contained in this book."
Rex Brady, President, Fuller Business Funding

"Marketing Magic cannot be measured by the price of the book – but by the benefit of the knowledge I gained by reading it."
Dennis Landenberger, Consultant

"OUTSTANDING! Finally a marketing book that actually shows you HOW to write a marketing plan, instead of just reciting statistic after statistic. Every cash flow consultant should read this book. It's written in plain and easy to understand English. Thanks again for being so willing to help others achieve what you have achieved."
Jeffrey J. Neal, Principal, Capital Options Group, LLC

"I've read Marketing Magic a couple of times now and it's given me a whole new perspective on how to do this business. In fact, I think I might give cold calling another chance now that I have some idea of what I should try to accomplish."
Peter Ilegan, Consultant

"Thanks once again for a book chock-full of stuff. Great read! I really enjoyed it and have recommended it to several people already! It's great for newbies and not-so-newbies to follow along: direct and to the point, what works and what doesn't, and ***how to do*** it. Knowing ***what*** to do is not the same as knowing ***how*** to do it. My favorite chapters were the ones that address how to deal with objections about cost, and the one on "Elephants, Rabbits and Quails". It made me re-think, and I'm now in the process of refining some of my own plans and projections."
Marguerite S. Cueto, Axis Financial Network

DASH POINT PUBLISHING

Order Form

Fax Orders: (253) 719-8132
Include this completed form.

Telephone Orders: (866)-676-0966 – Toll Free!

Web Site Orders: www.DashPointPublishing.com

Email Orders: info@DashPointPublishing.com

Postal Orders: Dash Point Publishing, Inc.
P.O. Box 25591
Federal Way, WA 98093-2591

Please send the following resources:
_____
_____
_____
_____
_____
_____
_____
_____
_____
_____

Name _____
Address _____
City, State, Zip _____
Telephone _____
Email _____

Sales Tax: Please add 8.8% for products shipped to Washington state.

Payment:
☐ Visa ☐ MasterCard *Make checks to:*
☐ Discover ☐ AmEx ☐ Check Dash Point Publishing

Card # _____
Name on card _____ Exp. date _____